Income Anywhere!

FOURTH EDITION

The Ultimate Guide for How to Full-time RV and Support Your Nomadic Lifestyle

BY RENE AGREDANO AND JIM NELSON

@LiveWorkDream

https://liveworkdream.com

INCOME ANYWHERE!
FOURTH EDITION
by Rene Agredano and Jim Nelson
@LiveWorkDream
https://liveworkdream.com

ISBN: 978-1-7334689-3-0

Published in the United States by:
Agreda Communications
240 Rainbow Dr., #14065
Livingston, TX 77399
https://agreda.com

Cover & Interior Design: Jim Nelson

© 2006-2022 Agreda Communications. The brands LIVE WORK DREAM, TRIPAWD/s, and BE MORE DOG are registered trademarks of Agreda Communications. All Rights Reserved. Content herein is copyrighted and may not be distributed nor duplicated without express written permission of the authors.

DISCLAIMER: We (The Authors) are not lawyers, certified financial planning experts, nor licensed business professionals. All information provided herein is based only on our own experiences running our businesses and those of other work-from-anywhere entrepreneurs. No amount of income generated from use of this book is implied nor guaranteed. This information is not a substitute for your own due diligence which may include professional legal or financial advice.

Always seek the advice of legal counsel and financial advisors prior to making any financial decisions for your life or business. Never implement legal nor financial advice based on something you read in this book or in anything Agreda Communications publishes without consulting your business advisors.

We do not guarantee that the information presented herein will create financial and professional success. There is absolutely no assurance made of any outcome whatsoever. Neither safety nor efficacy is stated nor implied, directly or indirectly. Rene Agredano and Jim Nelson are not responsible nor liable, directly or indirectly, for any form of damages whatsoever resulting from the use (or misuse) of information contained in or implied by the information available at the agreda.com or liveworkdream websites, or within the pages of this electronic or printed document. By viewing this material, you agree to this statement.

ABOUT THIS BOOK

This book includes hundreds of references linked to informative articles, books, apps, and other helpful resources. Text links highlighted like this indicate active hyperlinks available in the interactive e-book version available.

Save 50% OFF e-book with Coupon Code: PAPERBACK
Only at: https://liveworkdream.com/shop

NOTE: It is our goal with this book to provide you with ideas, tips, and resources that can help you earn the income you need to support your dream lifestyle – from anywhere! It is up to you to make those dreams come true.

We hope you'll share your successes and challenges with us by tagging **@LiveWorkDream** on your favorite social media platforms.

As a positive force in the Workamping community for many years now, this professional duo continuously shares quality, how-to information via their books, website, and other media. ***They don't just write about it; they live it too. This guide won't steer you wrong.***
– JODY ANDERSON DUQUETTE
  EXECUTIVE DIRECTOR, WORKAMPER NEWS

I think what you're doing is cool.
– DAVE RAMSEY, THE DAVE RAMSEY SHOW

You guys are the OGs of full-time RVing.
– JASON EPPERSON, RV MILES PODCAST

CONTENTS

PREFACE 1
   Signs from the Universe Exist. Pay Attention.. 2

INTRODUCTION 7
   About Us: Who Are Jim and Rene? 7

HITTING THE ROAD 11
  3 Top Tips for Nomadic Independence 11
  Preparing to Hit the Road 17
     Prepare Your Mind 18
  Prepare your finances 32
     Choosing Your RV: Keep it Simple 34
     Budget the Easy Way (with YNAB!) 37

WORKAMPING 42
  How to Support Your Lifestyle with Workamping 43
     What is Workamping? 44
     What Kinds of Workamping Jobs Exist? 46
     Our First Steps to Workamping 49
     Discovering Workamping Alternative Currency ... 50
     Workamping Disadvantages 51
  How to Find Workamping Jobs on the Road 52
     Theme Park Workamping. 56
     Ranch and Farm Workamping Jobs 57
     Work in the Cannabis Industry 59
     "Offbeat" Workamping Opportunities 60
     Workamping As a Gate Guard. 61
     More Tips to Find Your Ideal Workamping Job. ... 63
  Other Workamping Considerations. 66
     Reach Beyond Your Comfort Zone. 66
     How to Mix Business and Workamping. 67

    Workamping with Pets 67
    Choosing a Workamping Location 68
    Let's Talk About Workamping Pay 69
    Do You Need to Get It in Writing? 70
    What About Taxes? 72

MAKING MONEY 77
  More Ways To Support Your Nomadic Lifestyle 77
  Is Remote Employment in Your Future? 77
    How to Find Remote Jobs 79
  "Home-Based Business" Opportunities 85
    Watch Out for Scams! 86
  The Gig Economy 94
    Join the Talent Marketplace 106
    Freelance Work Resources for Side-Hustle Jobs 110
    Micro Jobs and the Truth About Taking Surveys 114

SELF-EMPLOYMENT 123
  Should You Start Your Own Business? 123
    Why Self-employment Is the Way to Go 123
    Small Business You Can Do Anywhere 125
    Step 1: Find Your Purpose 127
    Attributes of Successful Self-Employed People 129
  Everyone Is an Expert 131
    Narrow Your Niche to Succeed .132
  New Business Considerations 136
    Don't Reinvent the Wheel 138
    Marketing Your New Business .142
  E-commerce – Setting Up Your Online Storefront 146
    Use existing E-commerce Tools 146

- Sell Handmade Crafts to a Global Audience.........148
- Open an Amazon Store 151
- Open Your Own Shop Online 155
- Be Creative: Sell Your Designs Online 159
- Sell Your Music Online 161
- Making Money from Your Blog........................163
  - Content Marketing Through Blogging 163
  - Our Primary Niche Blog Success 166
  - How to Get Started Blogging.....................168
  - Content Is Key 170
  - Blog Revenue Takes Time, Be Patient 172
  - How to Monetize Your Blog with Your Writing.....176
  - Earning Blog Income with Affiliate Advertising........179
  - More Blog Income from Pay Per Click Advertising....193
  - Develop Brand Engagement Relationships 197
- WordPress E-commerce: Set Up Your Blog Shop.......199
- Profit from Your Expertise.........................205
  - What Is A Coach?................................205
  - Build Your Community, Grow Your Business 206
  - Enter the World of Self-Publishing 218

CONCLUSION 223
- Yes, You Can Design Your Own Nomadic Lifestyle! 223

APPENDIX..226
- Questions To Ask About Your Workamping Job 226
- Pyramid Style Schemes vs. Legitimate Revenue Sharing Businesses 229
- Recommended Reading 231

Be More Dog: Learning to Live in the Now............232

PREFACE

As we write this it's Fall, 2021 and just when we thought the U.S. was climbing out of the COVID-19 pandemic, SURPRISE! The Delta – and then Omicron – variant strikes. Currently, our carefree nomadic future is uncertain. But is this any different than life during the Before Times? Not a chance. We weren't fortune tellers then and we aren't now.

Being full-time RVers since 2007 has prepared us for the unexpected and it can do the same for you. The nomadic life teaches that we can never be 100% certain what's around the bend. A desire to experience never-ending travel means constantly accepting a level of uncertainty between Point A and Point B. Whether plans go off as expected or totally off the rails, you continuously hope for the best but prepare for the worst. And you always save your pennies for the inevitable rainy day.

The pandemic is one of the best examples of how the nomadic lifestyle can make you a stronger, smarter person living a more fulfilled life. In our case, we were already comfortable with uncertainty when the world learned the word "COVID." The experience wasn't a picnic, but we already knew how to quickly adapt and evolve with changing the circumstances. Did it shield us from the worst effects of the pandemic? Not a chance.

In March 2020 we scrambled for a place to stay when RV resorts shut down around the nation. Despite our hyper-vigilant isolation efforts, both of us had contracted COVID that January. Our business took a hit, family relationships exploded, and like you, the situation forced us to re-evaluate what matters to us. We asked: what did we want to accomplish in an era of extreme uncertainty?

PREFACE

Finishing this book rose to the top of our to-do list because full-time travel has never been more popular than it is now. More people than ever are buying RVs, transitioning to vanlife or plotting global travel adventures. The smart ones are researching ways to work remotely and make money from anywhere. And, they are seeking a better way to earn a living, feel happier, and enjoy a more financially secure future. People who do their research before their bon voyage party have a better chance at achieving their full-time travel goals. Those who wait for Facebook to hand them answers, probably won't.

Over the years we have seen numerous working, full-time RV nomads come and go. Some give up full-timing and retreat to "the default life" because they miss being rooted in a stick house. But many just don't plan well and go broke. We don't want that to happen to you. Whether you want to travel for a season, a year or longer, this updated edition of *Income Anywhere!* explains dozens of ways you can support your travel habit. After 14+ years on the road, we are living proof that the methods in this book can support long-term travel. Read on and you'll have the information it takes to succeed.

Signs from the Universe Exist. Pay Attention.

Life is filled with coincidences. Most times we don't recognize them. If we do, rarely do we understand their connections to our life. But here's one that's easy to decipher: If you are reading this book, it's not a coincidence. It did not randomly fall onto your radar. Maybe your Google searches spawned an ad that enticed you to click, but even if you found it some other way, you are meant to read what's between the pages. The *Youniverse* wants you to create your dream life.

> *The coincidences or little miracles that happen every day of your life are hints that the universe has much bigger plans for you than you ever dreamed of for yourself.*
> – DEEPAK CHOPRA, *SYNCHRODESTINY*
>   HTTPS://AMZN.TO/3DMAHP7

Years ago, we didn't put much thought into coincidences and synchrodestiny. We were working to grow our first business together, but a parade of nomads enjoying offbeat lifestyles kept showing up in our life. One of the most inspirational was a 72-year old adventure writer who had taken two solo motorcycle trips around the world. Nomads like him were following their dreams in unconventional ways and their off-beat lifestyles ignited daydreams of hiking the Pacific Crest Trail, or taking a cross-country road trip.

But reality always set in. Bills needed paying and those crazy lifestyles were things **other** people did – not two responsible 30-something entrepreneurs like us! Full-time travel just didn't seem realistic or smart. Our eat-work-sleep-repeat daily grind was all we knew, until a series of sad events taught us the cold, hard truth: life is short.

Between 2001 and 2006, Jim's parents passed away. Then 9/11 happened. The dot com bust nearly destroyed our business. Rene was almost killed when a deer collided with her motorcycle. A 52-year old friend died from terminal brain cancer. And then, the biggest tragedy hit us in 2006. Our beloved dog Jerry needed a leg amputated because of terminal bone cancer.

Life beat the crap out of us in a very short amount of time. Jerry's diagnosis was the Universe's wake up call to create the life we always wanted.

Is the Universe sending you signals too?

We hope it doesn't take tragedy to get you on the path you want to follow. So please, don't wait. If the Universe is sending signs that your life needs a new direction, pay attention.

▶ What events led you to finding this book? Are they connected?
▶ Why did you click through and download this book?
▶ Who inspired you to consider the possibility of living differently?

Follow the signs, and start pursuing your dreams. Stop putting them away on the "someday" shelf of your life. Now is the time to create the reality you want. If you have no idea where to begin, relax. By the time you're done with this book, you will.

We also kicked off our lifestyle designs by learning from the experts. Back then, a few of our first reads included <u>Six Months Off</u>, <u>The Four-hour Workweek</u>, and <u>Smart Couples Finish Rich</u>. Later helpful books included <u>Start</u>, <u>The Slight Edge</u>, <u>Quitter</u>, and <u>The Total Money Makeover</u>.

We took our new knowledge and insights, unfurled a roll of packing paper, and started brainstorming. In a vision-board style collage, we pasted quotes, wrote our desires, needs, and wants onto the brown paper spread across our living room floor. The rough draft also included a <u>SWOT analysis</u> of our *Strengths, Weaknesses, Opportunities and Threats*. Finally, we categorized our traits, talents and skills. The vision of our new future as nomads became clear. (See <u>Hitting the Road</u> section for details.)

Today you can skip the kraft paper exercise and embrace web-based mindmapping tools like <u>Coggle</u> and <u>LucidChart</u> – among many others. But it doesn't really matter if you want to mind map or not—if you have read this far, you probably have what it takes to find enjoyable work that pays for a fulfilling, unconventional, nomadic life.

Don't think you have to follow exactly in our footsteps as you plan your future. Not everyone can or will make the same exact choices we do. If you have a family, or are a caregiver to a dependent, the roadmap to your dreams may be very different from ours. But no matter where you are in life today, you can still take steps to get closer to your dreams of tomorrow. Whatever your age, income, or life circumstances, you have it within you to create a plan for *your* ideal life.

RECOMMENDED READING

Read Start, Repeat (Book Review)
http://www.liveworkdream.com/2013/05/19/read-start-repeat/

Six Months Off
https://amzn.to/3zBq4YN

The Four-hour Workweek
https://amzn.to/33fLjD8

Smart Couples Finish Rich
https://amzn.to/3n80xkM

The Slight Edge
https://amzn.to/3JN1TeF

Quitter
https://amzn.to/31D6XRq

Free Agent Nation
https://amzn.to/35YjGAd

The Total Money Makeover: A Proven Plan for Financial Fitness
https://amzn.to/3FfnEjS

To access highlighted links throughout this book, Save 50% OFF the e-book with coupon code: PAPERBACK Only at: https://liveworkdream.com/shop

---

"Someday" is a disease that will take your dreams to the grave with you.

If the challenge we face doesn't scare us, then it's probably not that important.

– TIM FERRISS

❗ Reliable internet connectivity is a must-have for making a living on the road. You cannot rely only upon public wifi. Redundancy is the only true solution. Compare best mobile internet options:
https://bit.ly/rvinternetoptions

PREFACE

> ***To be truly challenging**, a voyage, like a life, must rest on a firm foundation of financial unrest . . . 'I've always wanted to sail to the South Seas, but I can't afford it.' What these men can't afford is not to go. They are enmeshed in the cancerous discipline of security. And in the worship of security we fling our lives beneath the wheels of routine. And before we know it our lives are gone.*
>
> *What does a man need, really need? A few pounds of food each day, heat and shelter, six feet to lie down in – and some form of working activity that will yield a sense of accomplishment. That's all, in the material sense, and we know it. But we are brainwashed by our economic system until we end up in a tomb beneath a pyramid of time payments, mortgages, preposterous gadgetry, playthings that divert our attention from the sheer idiocy of the charade.*
>
> *The years thunder by. The dreams of youth grow dim where they lie caked in dust on the shelves of patience. Before we know it, the tomb is sealed.*
>
> *Where, then, lies the answer? In choice. Which shall it be: bankruptcy of purse or bankruptcy of life?*
>
> –AUTHOR STERLING HAYDEN
> FROM HIS 1976 NOVEL, *VOYAGE*
> HTTPS://AMZN.TO/3F9Z8K3

INTRODUCTION

About Us: Who Are Jim and Rene?

"You guys have been doing this for a **very** long time… you two are the OGs of full-time RVing." A popular RVing podcast host told us this during our June, 2020 interview. We weren't sure if it was a compliment or an unintended jab at our ages, but we burst out loud laughing anyway.

Yes, that's us, the Original Gangstas of the nomadic lifestyle. We'll take the credit. After all, it was way back in 2006 when the wanderlust bug bit us. That was the dark ages of nomadic living, over a decade before the term "digital nomads" popped up. Comfortably settled and ingrained into the routine of our late 30s, we were self-employed entrepreneurs living in a remote, Northern California town known worldwide for pot growing and not much else. Living outside the box felt natural to us. Ironically, now we live *in* a box, but we'll get to that.

It all started in 1998, when we ditched our big city San Francisco life for remote Humboldt County. Our town was full of old hippies and offbeat folks with quirky, crunchy lifestyles we appreciated. Many were free-spirited, living off-grid and far from the beaten path. We loved the way they followed the beat of their own drum.

Meanwhile we grew our home-based marketing agency, Agreda Communications, into a full service print and publishing provider helping clients around the globe. We were self-employed, high-tech community leaders who lived and worked in a 3,700-square foot historic home office that we restored from the ground up. "Responsibility" was our badge of honor, and long hours in the office is how we earned it. Meanwhile our beloved "Chief Fun Officer" Jerry G. Dawg spent his days patiently waiting for the musical notes of our computers to shut down for the night. He lived for our Friday beach walks and the occasional backpacking trips we crammed into our busy schedule. There never seemed to be enough of those outings, but he never complained. Time whizzed by as we built our business, tossing aside our passions for "someday" and banking on a future without guarantees.

Everything changed in November, 2006 when Jerry was diagnosed with terminal bone cancer. To give him a better quality of life in the six months vets said he had left, surgeons amputated his front left leg. We grieved for his limb loss, but we quickly saw that Jerry didn't care about losing a leg or the grim prognosis. He recuperated without a whimper or a whine. It was his way of showing us that <u>all we have is Now</u>. That dog did not feel sad, and he wasn't embarrassed because he looked different. He just wanted to get on with life and enjoy every day to the fullest while showing us how to **Be More Dog**.

Each day with our wise leader started feeling like a gift. It didn't take long to realize that our gritty work schedule was stealing precious time away from him. A major life change needed to happen, or we would be filled with regret when Jerry said goodbye. It was all the motivation we needed to kick-start our crazy traveling dreams.

First, we drew up a plan to sell our business. The proceeds would pay for a year off from work. Then we could give Jerry one final gift – an open ended, cross country road trip! He loved seeing new places and camping as much as we did. We decided that spending his final months traveling was the least we could do to pay him back for all the love and wisdom he gave to us.

Six months after creating our plan, we hit the road in a new RV to see North America with our three-legged Zen master. It was the best decision we ever made. The new lifestyle gave us two amazing years, during which Jerry helped us find our purpose. That bittersweet journey led us to create the Tripawds pet amputation support community. And although he's no longer with us physically, his presence still guides us every day. Our road trip continues today as we roam while doing fulfilling, meaningful work that supports ourselves now, and into our future.

No longer tied to the stick house way of life, our office view often looks out on some of the most beautiful places in North America. How do we pay for it?

- Rene works as a writer for online publications and trade magazines. She also makes jewelry from her mobile metalworking studio.
- Jim is also a writer, and graphic designer. He's a WordPress guru helping select clients with website development, e-commerce, and marketing.
- We share our nomadic adventures, full-time RVing tips, and product reviews at liveworkdream.com.
- But our true passion is Tripawds, the largest online support community for three-legged dogs and cats, and their people. As part of it, we also manage the 501c3 Tripawds Foundation, which helps concerned pet parents with many free resources, veterinary financial aid, and direct-assistance programs for animal amputation recovery and care.

And yes, we do it all from our mobile headquarters.

Fifteen years ago if you had told us this would be our life, we would not have believed it. But if we can follow our passions and make money on the road, you can too! Not all of what we discuss in this book will work for everyone. But some of it is sure to be applicable to someone – even you! If you incorporate just one or two of the proven strategies we've discovered into your life, you're better off than you were before you picked up a copy. Even if you decide not to travel at all, you'll know more of what it takes to be self-sufficient anywhere and thrive in today's ruthless economy.

INTRODUCTION

Rene and Jim with Jerry – Alpine Loop, Colorado

> *You can only become truly accomplished at something you love. Don't make money your goal. Instead, pursue the things you love doing, and then do them so well that people cannot take their eyes off you.*
> – MAYA ANGELOU

With Wyatt Ray – Quartzsite, Arizona

liveworkdream.com

HITTING THE ROAD

3 Top Tips for Nomadic Independence

A location independent lifestyle teaches so much about financial independence. Working on the road is a continuous process of evaluating what matters to you personally, spiritually, and financially. Always make an effort to keep your goals on track, but don't forget to have fun too.

Let's dive into some important lessons we've learned in our 15 years on the road, starting with the three most important:

1. Full-time RVing without Debt is Real Freedom

Our travels with Jerry gave us the time of our lives. But it wasn't without worry. Living off our savings during that first year on the road was stressful. Without any sort of steady income, Rene constantly worried about more money going out than coming in.

Then in late 2007 while traveling down the East Coast, we met a family of five living on the road. This was practically unheard of back then. It was an encounter that permanently changed our financial picture for the better. The couple owned a paid-for RV, and was full-timing with zero debt. They introduced us to the teachings of financial guru and debt-free evangelist, <u>Dave Ramsey</u>, and even gifted us his most popular book, "<u>Total Money Makeover</u>."

Being without debt felt unrealistic at the time. We had an RV loan, and used credit cards for everything, even though we paid them off every month. Both of us assumed debt was a normal part of life. But Dave Ramsey taught us an important lesson when it comes to debt: "normal" is dumb.

> *"Normal" people carry so much debt that they can't make any major life changes unless they earn more money.*
> — DAVE RAMSEY

Most people are trapped in a job they hate, because they are mainly working to pay down a credit card, car loan, or mortgage balance. If that job goes away and they can't pay their bills, it's a catastrophe. Ramsey taught us that even though we paid our credit cards off every month, we were still in debt like most people. If our income disappeared, we would have a very hard time paying off the balance.

Ramsey teaches that being "a slave to your lender" puts a dark karmic cloud over your head. The weight of it prevents you from living a life of true freedom until that debt cloud is completely gone.

The idea of living debt free opened our eyes. We learned that putting your financial situation at risk by living beyond your means burdened with debt is risky. And RV living in debt without a traditional job and housing situation is even scarier. We wondered why anyone would endanger their well-being for the sake of material things that ultimately don't make you happier or any more content.

That was our light bulb moment. If we got rid of debt, we wouldn't need to work as hard just to pay the bills. If we wanted to keep the road trip going and enjoy more free time, we had to be willing to live debt-free. In return we could pursue interests that might not pay with money, but rewarded us with a happier, spiritually wealthy existence.

Once we started following Ramsey's teachings, our financial picture improved greatly. We've now been on the road through two economic recessions and the COVID-19 pandemic. We not only survived, but thrived because we weren't weighed down with debt. By creating and sticking to a monthly budget, living within our means, and paying cash for everything we are building financial wealth through good economic times and bad. Sure, we don't have the newest truck, fanciest RV, or best tech gear. But staying out of debt is the primary tool that gives us the ability to enjoy this lifestyle we love so much. We are much happier and feel more secure living debt-free.

2. Everyone Needs Multiple Revenue Streams

Relying on one source of income is a fool's game. Nomadic or not, it doesn't matter if you're an employee or self-employed weirdos like us. Everyone needs multiple revenue streams to survive and thrive in a permanent era of layoffs, downsizings, and mergers.

Lifestyle design expert Tim Ferriss teaches about the importance of creating multiple revenue streams in his book, The 4-Hour Workweek. Create multiple revenue streams for maximum financial security, he advises. That doesn't mean holding down multiple jobs. Instead, build wealth through multiple revenue streams while focusing efforts on the primary method which earns the most profit.

In our early years on the road we toyed with different revenue streams. Our best money-making sources came from Rene's freelance writing and Jim's marketing consulting. Meanwhile Tripawds grew into our main labor of love so we focus on building the community, while bringing in money from those other methods. In coming chapters we get into more details about how we did it.

Build one main income source, nurture smaller ones.

Tim Ferriss' book is geared toward being self-employed, but you can also build multiple revenue streams even if you're a company employee. For instance, first land a great job that you know you'll enjoy, and can do anywhere. Then, focus on nurturing various smaller side-hustles that can serve as a back-up if your main income source dries up. Build up that campfire. Try different things to stoke the flames. Blow on the money sources that glow the hottest.

Let the others burn out. Soon you will know what works best to keep your wheels rolling.

Think you're up to the challenge of being a full-time entrepreneur? Establish a main business model centered upon your strongest skills. Then create smaller ventures based on automated processes that help you get the maximum amount of income from the main venture.

EXAMPLE 1: Start an online niche business for a specific interest that you are passionate about. Sell multiple products, instructional videos, and/or coaching centered on the same interest. Supplement profits with affiliate sales of related products.

EXAMPLE 2: Create a physical product that meets a very specific demand. Develop a brand around that niche to attract loyalists who support your sales through community building and social sharing. Expand to offer branded apparel, books and related products.

> *Where a lot of people mess up [in attempting to create passive income] is they try to build a business or create a product that serves everybody, and by trying to serve everybody, you serve nobody. You have to specialize and niche down and find a market with a pain point that you, based on your experience, based on your education and based on your passion, can help.*
> – PAT FLYNN

There are no bad business ideas, just poor follow-through. If you have a small business idea, one of the best books we recommend is <u>Will It Fly?</u> In this business startup workbook, Pat Flynn guides you through the steps necessary to determine if your business model is viable enough to get off the ground.

Most importantly of all, he teaches how to save yourself the precious time, effort and investment by following through on your research phase before launching any project you're crazy about.

3. Follow Your Passion *and* Your Purpose for Success

You've probably heard the phrase "follow your passion and the money will follow." We hate to break it to you, but success doesn't happen quite like that. Whether you choose to get a remote job with a company you're crazy about, or take The Big Leap into self-employment life, the ability to generate an income from doing something you love requires skill, passion and purpose.

EXAMPLE: By day you work at a boring desk job, but during your spare time you feed your artistic side by creating beautiful stained glass hummingbird feeders. The art of crafting them and seeing birds drink from your unique designs makes your heart sing.

Friends and family tell you the feeders are great, and that you should sell them as a business. You're tempted to do it, but don't quit your day job yet. That passion to create bird feeders isn't the only ingredient to bring home an income. You also need purpose.

What do we mean by purpose?

To stand out from the other bird feeders, yours must fulfill a very specific need, either for the birds, the people, or ideally both. After all, the people are your customers, not the birds.

For example, your feeders can make it easier to nourish the birds. They help people spend less time maintaining the feeder and more time birdwatching. Perhaps you develop a recipe for organic nectar that is actually healthy for hummingbirds, included free with every purchase. That's your purpose! Making life better for both species is your product's "unique selling proposition" that separates it from competition. Market your above-average feeders to the passionate audience in search of better birdwatching and healthier bird populations. Your product will be much more attractive to them than all the other usual feeders on store shelves.

In our case, we found our purpose at Tripawds by helping others coping with amputation recovery and care for their beloved pets. We never want anyone to ever feel as lost and alone as we did when receiving a limb cancer diagnosis for their dog. From the start, our goal was to provide the information and support people need at a time like that. Yes, we earn a small income by selling mobility gear and information products. But it is only by serving others that we love what we do, and feel more fulfilled by doing it on a daily basis.

Making, teaching, or selling something solely because you love it, isn't enough to earn a steady income. Whether you decide to start a business or work for someone else, aim for creating a product or service that serves a purpose larger than yourself. When you are driven to serve others, the time you spend doing it is more fulfilling than just chasing after a dollar. Get yourself to that place where "work" doesn't feel like work. When you are helping others meet a specific need, you will be surprised at how many new opportunities appear and help you make more money doing what you love.

> *The secret is to make other people happy."*
> –DEEPAK CHOPRA

These three key lessons have helped us grow as full-time RVers, digital nomads, entrepreneurs, and all around better human beings. They've enabled us to maintain our lifestyle exactly how we like it. Staying out of debt and juggling multiple income sources isn't always the easiest path to take. But living by these philosophies allows us to enjoy life on our terms. We are confident that following these paths can do the same for you.

RECOMMENDED READING

Below are some authors who share wisdom and life philosophies that we find helpful:

The Total Money Makeover by Dave Ramsey
https://amzn.to/3E850u3

The Ultimate Retirement Guide for 50+: Winning Strategies to Make Your Money Last a Lifetime by Suze Orman
https://amzn.to/3jqhyoC

The Four Hour Workweek by Tim Ferriss
https://amzn.to/3jpvgl6

You Need a Budget by Jessee Meecham
https://amzn.to/3B20RWA

Will It Fly? by Pat Flynn
https://amzn.to/3b0BHwU

Start: Punch Fear in the Face, Escape Average and Do Work that Matters by Jon Acuff
https://amzn.to/3m0JgKk

The Big Leap: Conquer Your Hidden Fear and Take Life to the Next Level by Gay Hendricks
https://amzn.to/3niz53e

Synchrodestiny : Harnessing the Infinite Power of Coincidence to Create Miracles by Deepak Chopra
https://amzn.to/3b0nfF8

"A sure-fire way to predict the future is to take no action at all. When you do nothing, you get nothing."
— PAT FLYNN, WILL IT FLY?

Preparing to Hit the Road

The idea of breaking our routine to hit the road first occurred during some mindless channel surfing. A short-lived show called "Radical Sabbatical" got our wheels turning. Each 30-minute segment told the story of someone bored with their career and searching for a dramatic life change. The show led people on a journey to discover their next big thing.

Watching those people work hard to make their dreams happen provided inspiration we needed to kick-start our own dreams. We weren't enjoying our business all that much anymore, and Jerry's diagnosis was the catalyst that made us decide to put the business and our home on the market.

We knew it could take a year to recuperate from the decade we spent working so hard to build our business. So we agreed that one year of freedom would help us pinpoint our future goals. By roaming the country in an RV, we could see other successful self-employment situations, and experience North America's best sights at the same time.

But first we had to figure out how to pay for it. We could have lived off the proceeds of our house and business for two years, at most. But the thought of hemorrhaging a huge chunk of our life savings made us both uneasy. The same could be said by anyone without savings to throw at an open-ended road trip.

As Dave Ramsey says, "**the difference between a dream and a goal is a plan.**" We had a goal, and we had a plan. This book outlines the steps we took to plan our escape from the default life. Each step was an ingredient in a recipe that helped us stay on the road without going broke.

Planning is the best way for anyone who wants to do the same. If anyone tells you, "Just do it" or "Go for it, you'll figure out how to make it work"--run! We have seen enough of that bad advice on social media to know that it usually ends in disaster.

Prepare Your Mind

Brainstorming about your road trip dreams and hopes is a fun way to explore your desire to leave the default life behind. Here are some tips from our brainstorming phase:

▶ Jot your ideas on a "dream board" of <u>giant sticky notes</u>. Leave them up in a place where you can see your dreams and add notes every day.

INCOME ANYWHERE!

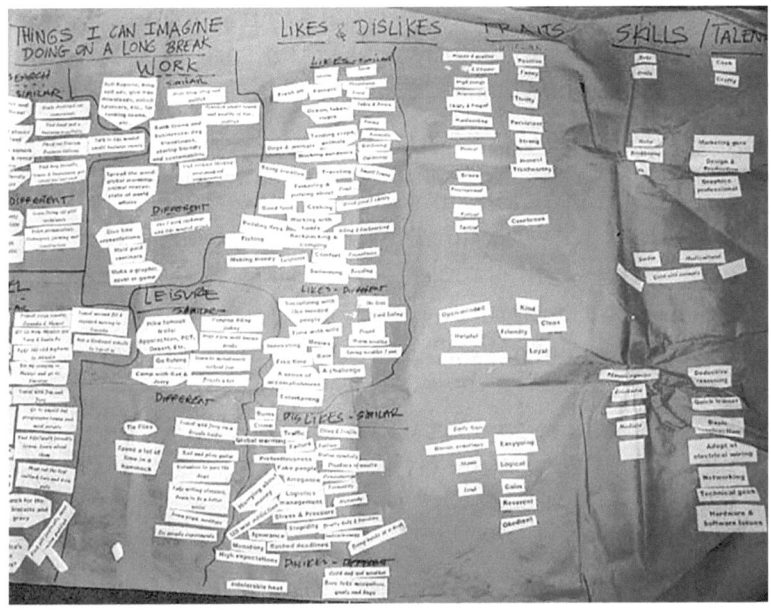

The brainstorming board that kicked off our nomadic journey.

- Create categories that describe the various concepts relating to your new lifestyle. For example, if you want to full-time RV, make a category for "Places to See" and another for "Bucket List Activities."
- Get everyone involved to jot down and categorize their goals, desires, likes, dislikes, fears and expectations about this life change.
- User small color-coded stickies to represent different ideas or individuals. Move them around your dream board to further categorize ideas and actions.
- Next, review those concepts. Look for common trends and differences.

Your goal with this brainstorming project is to work toward a complete understanding of how everyone involved envisions this new lifestyle. Aim to reach an agreement of understanding about all aspects of a journey, from the type of RV to destinations, and how you'll earn money, to the fun activities on everyone's bucket list.

Questions to Ask Yourself

- Are you more comfortable staying in one place for extended visits? Or do you want to move around a general geographic region?
- Does the thought of staying in a big city, five-star RV park appeal to you? Or are you a backcountry camper?
- Do you want to connect with other like-minded people? Or get away from civilization?
- What geographical and climate regions appeal to you?
- Where are the places you want to avoid?
- Do you have kids who will be home schooled?
- Will your travels have a goal, like traveling to historic sites to educate your kids?
- Do you prefer traveling back roads – or getting from Point A to Point B in the least amount of time?
- Would you prefer a strict travel itinerary to visit every place on your "must-see" list? Or would you rather let the road lead you to unexpected treasures?
- When are the best times to visit the things, people and places you want to see?
- Will you keep your home, put your stuff in storage, or get rid of everything?
- Are you able to make frequent stops while traveling to different locations, for getting a snack or using the restroom? Or do you want everything at your fingertips when rolling down the road?
- How much vehicle and RV maintenance can you do yourself?

- Do you think you can handle living with your spouse or family in such a small space, all the time?
- What is your savings and income situation? Will that cover your expected expenses (e.g.; rent, fuel, food, maintenance, repairs)?
- Can you work your current job remotely?
- Do you want to start a business on the road?
- Are you willing to take on extra work that will help you save money, such as seasonal jobs at campgrounds?

Flexibility is Key in this Lifestyle

Everyone's brainstorming sessions look different. But one thing that everyone needs to possess is a willingness to be flexible. Whether you're single, part of a couple or a big happy family, full-time RVers must be able to adapt to changing and sometimes tough circumstances. This is especially true when you're still learning the ins and outs of dump stations, backing up, and navigation.

No matter how long you're on the road, it feels like a huge accomplishment if things go according to plan. And even when they don't, you need to accept that it's still a good day. One of our favorite mantras is:

<u>The Situation is the Boss.</u>

If you choose this lifestyle, the predictable days of living the default life in suburbia becomes a thing of the past. Every turn brings another new experience and in the early days, plenty of frustration too.

In the heat of the moment, can you accept and adapt, or stay stuck in a bad attitude? Can you embrace the unknown and unexpected, or will misadventure leave you stressed and angry?

This is the beauty, and the challenge, of the nomadic lifestyle. Even the rough times can teach us so much, and make us stronger people. But if you cannot be a duck on the water and allow the drops to roll off your back while paddling upstream, you will probably not enjoy living this unpredictable, exciting lifestyle.

> *At its core Adventure is the willingness to commit to an uncertain outcome with an open heart and an open mind.*
> – MATT WALKER, ADVENTURE IN EVERYTHING

RECOMMENDED READING
The Situation is the Boss
https://liveworkdream.com/2018/05/16/the-situation-is-the-boss/

Friends, Family, Pets, Health and "Stuff"

Nobody lives in a vacuum. Whether you are solo, travel with pets or family, most RVers have to consider other factors that affect their road trip plans and ultimately, their state of mind. Here are some of the most common issues that affect all nomads.

Friends and family might not understand your decision

You may find that the people you once considered allies just don't support you in your dream. Once you announce your plans to hit the road, some friends and family won't understand why you want to live so differently. They'll panic at your sudden urge to give up your career, walk away from the false security of a "stable" job, or take your kids on the road. You may become the black sheep, the neglectful parent, slacker, or family freak who sticks out from the rest.

Are you strong enough to ignore the negativity of those who are closest to you? Can you make your own way without allowing the naysayers to bring you down? This decision is simple for some freedom seekers. But many feel the loss of connection may be too much to risk. If that's you, don't worry, you are not alone. There is a massive growing community of fellow nomads who do understand.

Some people, however, simply don't get it. And they never will – even after they see how happy it makes you and how much fun you're having. If you're encountering resistance or aren't sure this lifestyle is for you, seek support from people who share your thinking about the nomadic lifestyle.

- RVing groups like Escapees, Xscapers and many other online forums are all filled with full-timing members ready to offer insight. Their experience and opinions offer support and encouragement for aspiring road trippers.
- Get active in online RVer communities and start building real-life networks of support. You'll find Facebook groups for every mode of travel, from backpacking and vandwelling to fifth wheel trailers, Class A rigs, and toy haulers.
- Turn to niche websites with well moderated discussion forums for the best sense of community and helpful advice, without the attitude and distraction of social media.

By connecting with others in a safe place around a common purpose, you will get honest feedback, inspiration, and strength from like minded people who share and support your dream.

Rethink what "community" means to you

Leaving our old home town of Eureka, California, was tough. We loved that small-town feel of living in a remote area. It provided the strongest sense of community we had ever enjoyed. We were very active in the local business community for ten years, and had a strong network of friends. With a large house and home office downtown, we often hosted popular parties and felt like we were part of something bigger than ourselves. Leaving all that behind was the hardest part of hitting the road.

We briefly considered returning to Eureka during our first visit back. A couple years later, the thought of settling down once again crossed our minds. But after experiencing so many other awesome communities in our travels, the desire to explore more of them was irresistible.

Home is where we park it.

Over the years we've discovered that this lifestyle isn't for everyone. Full-timers do miss out on many events, holidays and festivities with friends and family members. Sure, nomadic folks can travel to many gatherings in their old home towns, but that's not always easy, affordable, or convenient. Lots of travelers eventually discover they miss the sense of community they once enjoyed. Persoanlly, we have come to enjoy the camaraderie shared by the majority of full-time RVers. And we welcome every chance we get to grow our virtual community – both online, and with new nomads we meeet.

For some, the FOMO (fear of missing out) after leaving "home" or family behind is just too much to stand. Over the years, we have seen dozens of full-timers hang up the keys for this reason.

Kids and Family Considerations

In 1972, Escapees RV Club founders Joe and Kay Peterson went full-timing with their two kids. Back then, there were no support groups to help trailblazers like them with homeschooling and other family challenges. But today, there are numerous full-timing families sharing their stories on the web. We aren't parents of human kids, so we can't give any advice in this area. But the internet is full of people who can. If you're thinking about hitting the road with kids, join a support community or talk with other parents who are doing it.

The following are just a few popular family RVing resources and blogs. Search "rving with kids" for many more.

FAMILY RVING RESOURCES

Fulltime Families RV Club
https://www.fulltimefamilies.com/

Families on the Road
https://www.familiesontheroad.com/

DitchingSuburbia
http://ditchingsuburbia.com/

Home Meets Road
http://homemeetsroad.com/

Neales...on wheels!
https://nealesonwheels.com/

Never Say Someday
http://neversaysomedayfamily.com/

The Camper House
https://thecamperhouse.com/

The Flying Hens
https://theflyinghens.com/

Traveling with Pets

Our dog Jerry was the inspiration for our road trip. He lived for the daily adventures and did great as a traveling dog. His successor Wyatt Ray was also an excellent co-pilot. But as a German Shepherd who lost a leg to neglect as a puppy, he had behavioral issues. For starters, he wasn't great with other dogs – especially the tiny white ones found in every RV park, often barking at the end of a long Flexi leash. Pets who have travel and socialization issues may make life on the road more challenging, but not impossible.

When we first adopted Wyatt, we weren't certain he would adapt well to life on the road. So we consulted with an animal behaviorist for a professional opinion. She told us that yes, a German Shepherd needs structure and strong pack leadership. But it didn't matter where we were while leading. He only wanted to be together with us, wherever we went.

If you're having second thoughts about traveling with pets, whatever you do, please DO NOT give them up just because you think they won't enjoy life on the road.

How to help a dog or cat adjust:

- ▶ Give your pets as much time as possible to become familiar with your new home on wheels. Take mini-road trips with their bed and toys inside the rig, even just around the block the first few times.
- ▶ Work with a good trainer to help your pet acclimate to travel and new situations with other dogs.
- ▶ Ask your vet to prescribe a motion sickness medication and anti-anxiety medication if your pet gets car sick.

How to keep up with vet care

Veterinary health care for your pets while traveling full-time is another major consideration. We've traveled for years with dogs. Both were amputees. One had cancer, the other developed various health issues in his senior years. There are a few things we suggest to ensure you have the best health care for your pets on the road, when you can no longer call your "regular" vet.

With your home on wheels, you have the luxury of traveling to find a good vet. We are huge fans of veterinary teaching hospitals. You'll often receive the best possible care from a team of doctors and students, and there are various leading facilities located all around the united states.

When searching for a vet, always look for the red AAHA logo on any vet clinic door or website. If you don't see it, ask if they are accredited by the American Animal Hospital Association when calling to find a clinic. Or, search the AAHA directory first to find clinics which are held to the highest standards of veterinary care.

Finally, we strongly suggest investing in pet health insurance. We have used it for various incidents and medical emergencies which otherwise would have been unaffordable. And, before selecting any pet insurance policy, the best thing you can do is request a full medical records review to avoid any preexisting condition surprises when filing a claim. For complete details, check out the various articles and interviews about pet insurance in our Tripawds blog.

Working on the road with pets

If you're not familiar with workamping, we have a full section on that coming up next. If you know you will try workamping with pets, you'll also need to keep their needs in consideration. Locking up a dog in an RV all day while you're at work or chaining them to a lead is NOT a great idea, especially in an RV park.

We've always had a dog while workamping at several different jobs. So we know that workamping and pets is not mutually exclusive. Most employers welcome pets, but many parks have breed or size restrictions. It takes time and effort to find the right workamping arrangement that keeps your pets happy, safe, and entertained while you're on duty.

If working from home, daily life may seem no different for pets in an RV if they are used to you doing that in your house or apartment. Only you know your pets better than anyone else. Most animals, especially dogs, are happiest with their humans no matter where they are. Some sacrifices need to be made to ensure their safety and well-being, but we think it's worth the trade off. You do not have to abandon your pets to fulfill your road trip dream!

RESOURCES FOR RVING WITH PETS

AAHA Clinic Directory
https://www.aaha.org/your-pet/hospital-locator/

Pet Insurance Articles & Interviews
https://tripawds.com/tag/pet-insurance/

Workamping with Pets
https://liveworkdream.com/2021/09/01/workamping-with-pets/

Dealing with Your Health Concerns

It's hard to think about health insurance premiums and plans when dreaming about a new adventure. But health care is a big part of all our lives, and without a decent plan to address unexpected or chronic health issues on the road, you will drive yourself right into bankruptcy.

When we started full-timing, we left behind the best primary care doctor we've ever had, as well as our favorite dentist, Jim's brother. Things got a little scary when Rene needed to go to urgent care less than two weeks into our adventure, but we quickly learned two important workarounds during stressful medical situations:

- Telemedicine subscription programs can keep you out of the hospital. <u>When we got COVID</u> in January 2020, two MDs coached us through Covid symptoms remotely via telemedicine. Their suggestions and prescriptions prevented an expensive urgent care clinic visit that would have provided the same information we received for our $15 monthly fee. Telemedicine plans are relatively cheap and easy to access with decent internet connectivity.
- If you do need to see a physician in person, urgent care clinics are practically on every corner. They aren't cheap, but if you need care they're a fast, easy option.

Unfortunately, over the years we have watched portable health insurance plan selections for RVers under 65 slowly disappear. If you have chronic health issues, finding good, regular medical care is going to be expensive and challenging.

Full-time RVers health care plans are not a fun topic and go beyond the scope of this book. But it's critical for you to know your options, so we published this blog post to address some workarounds:

Health Care Options for RVers
<u>https://liveworkdream.com/2021/01/20/full-time-rvers-health-care</u>

Downsizing: How to become a minimalist

There's no way to get around it: RVs are not built to accommodate the amount of stuff found in the typical stick house. There are two ways to deal with this limitation: detach yourself from stuff and get rid of it. Or pay money for the false sense of security that comes from locking your things away in a storage unit.

Downsizing and Detaching Considerations

As you look around your current home, it's easy to get overwhelmed by what to keep and what to toss. Don't panic. Take a deep breath and start with the reason for downsizing in the first place. Approach the process by asking yourself:

- Am I ready to try full-timing indefinitely?
- Do I want to try full-timing for one year, then reassess?

In our case, we thought we were only traveling for a year. We planned and budgeted for a year-long sabbatical. Afterward, we were going to "settle down" again somewhere else. We kept what we thought was necessary to set up our new home, wherever that might be. Keep reading for details about how *that* turned out.

If you're the type of person who believes you want a permanent change, get rid of everything you cannot afford to store. And when you think you've ditched enough stuff, get rid of some more.

For that pile of things you just cannot get rid of, remember there is a cost to keeping it. Is the cost of storing those items over a given amount of time going to exceed their value? If so, your money might be better spent by purchasing replacements someday, if and when you decide to stop RVing.

Best Downsizing Tips from Experts

It can take months and lots of time to downsize depending upon the amount of stuff you have accumulated. The topic of eliminating possessions has filled entire books and websites like <u>Becoming Minimalist</u>. We won't reinvent the wheel, so instead we'll just point you to a couple of our favorite resources.

RECOMMENDED READING

Minimalism: Live a Meaningful Life
https://amzn.to/3qsmRlv

The Joy of Less, A Minimalist Living Guide: How to Declutter, Organize, and Simplify Your Life
https://amzn.to/3oiZIW5

RESOURCES FOR SELLING STUFF

Ebay
https://www.ebay.com/

Facebook Marketplace
https://www.facebook.com/marketplace

Craig's List
https://craigslist.org

Decluttr – The smart way to sell CDs, books, and tech.
https://www.decluttr.com/

Mercari – Get the app to sell almost anything.
https://www.mercari.com/

Poshmark – Sell fashion, home decor, and more.
https://poshmark.com/

Sell new and used wedding dresses:
Stillwhite: https://www.stillwhite.com/
Once Wed: https://www.oncewed.com/

Replacements – Sell china, crystal and dinnerware.
https://www.replacements.com/sell-to-us

Swappa – Sell used computers, game consoles, and home tech.
https://swappa.com/

Worthy – Sell jewelry and watches
https://www.worthy.com/

Offer Up – The simpler way to sell locally.
https://offerup.com/

Our Storage Wars Experience

Two garage sales after deciding to hit the road full-time, we boxed up our remaining possessions, called the movers and had them put our stuff into storage. With a 3700 sq. ft. home/office, we had a lot of stuff. As the large moving van drove off to their storage facility, we *thought* we had downsized.

Then two years later in 2009, we purchased a mountain property where we planned to spend summers in Colorado. When we went to retrieve our belongings, we were horrified at all the crap we saved! We even had to donate some items that wouldn't fit in the moving truck we rented. But we had everything we needed to furnish our small cabin. This would have been fine if we were "settling down" like we assumed we would. We didn't.

In 2017 we sold the mountain retreat we called Jerry's Acres. We had yet another yard sale, and more downsizing. This time, we fit our remaining earthly possessions into a 5x7 storage locker. This was the downsizing we should have done the first time around.

Today, we own nothing more than some items with sentimental value which we plan to enjoy in our senior years. Some people are brave enough to get rid of everything and anything that won't fit in their RV. But since ours is only 27-feet long, without any real basement storage, we opted to save only the most important things that matter to us.

A Bigger "Storage Unit" Investment

The storage bill for our remaining possessions was less than $75 a month, but we hated paying it. In 2021, we wanted more than a storage unit. We wanted an investment. One of our favorite places in the country is Fort Collins, Colorado, so we purchased a small duplex house knowing that someday when we hang up the keys, we want to live in this vibrant city. The house has two residences, a garage, RV parking, and a consistent rental income source.

Today, our "storage unit" is an income generating rental property and our official residence. We are still full-timing, but as Colorado residents. As a bonus, we have better health care too. At least now when another pandemic strikes – or this one gets worse, again – we have a safe place to park, near all the amenities and health care providers we may need.

RECOMMENDED READING

Six Months Off
https://amzn.to/3F4eq9R

Live Your Road Trip Dream
https://amzn.to/3fHEsXf

Downsized? Who, Us?
https://liveworkdream.com/2009/08/21/downsized-who-us/

Our Downsizing and Decluttering Evolution
https://liveworkdream.com/2017/09/06/downsizing-and-decluttering/

Why We Chose Our Colorado Domicile
https://liveworkdream.com/2021/03/31/health-care-for-nomads/

Ready for the Next Pandemic? (Spoiler Alert: It's Coming)
https://www.infectioncontroltoday.com/view/ready-for-the-next-pandemic-spoiler-alert-it-s-coming-

Prepare your finances

Whether we are self-employed or drawing a paycheck from an employer, all of us are at the mercy of the economy, global pandemics, and climate change. Many people learned this the hard way in the 2007 recession. That's when millions of folks got caught with their pants down after years of living beyond their means. And now, it's happening again. People are hurting economically, or losing their jobs. And too many are buying into the Nomadland myth. They believe that by converting a van or buying a cheap RV, you can automatically enjoy an easier, cheaper life than before. This might be the case for those who plan and save enough. But not for people already living on the edge.

Once on the road, many quickly learn another hard lesson: **Living in an RV is NOT always cheaper than living in a stick house.**

The nomadic lifestyle can eliminate certain expenses associated with the default life. But being a full-time RVer is not always cheaper than living in a stick house. Sure, you will spend less money for some things. But as a full-timer you will spend way more on others, like fuel and vehicle maintenance. With a home on wheels, you will always be at the mercy of keeping your vehicle running in good shape, and property owners who do or don't want you to park on their land, or RV parks charging the most they can for rent.

Don't post on social media and ask, "How much does it cost to live on the road?" Ask ten RVers, and you'll get ten different answers. Instead, stop and ask yourself if your definition of "expensive" or "cheap" is always the same as that of someone else? Nope! Whether you become a vandweller or a motorcoach owner, the costs for full-time RVing fluctuate wildly from person to person.

What one person believes is frugal, the other one sees as extravagant. The only way for you to know if you can afford this lifestyle is to understand these things *before* you hit the road:

▶ How much does it cost for you to live your life the way you currently do now?
▶ How much it will cost to maintain and move your RV?
▶ How much could it cost to camp the way you want to camp?

If you don't have a good grip on these answers, you may be in for a rude awakening. To keep your wheels turning:

1. Stay away from consumer debt, especially RV loans.
2. Budget and keep your spending under control.
3. Build multiple income streams that enable you to pay your living expenses, save money for emergencies, and grow a retirement fund.

Work on these three habits and you will have the tools necessary to survive and thrive in any economy or lifestyle – especially the full-time RVing one. Let's dig into these topics a little more.

Choosing Your RV: Keep it Simple

Amazon is full of books about how to choose your RV. We won't reinvent the wheel, so here's a summary of our own personal philosophy about deciding what is the best kind of RV to full-time in...for you.

Can you afford to maintain your RV? The older the RV, or the more options and mechanical systems in any rig, the more things can and will eventually go wrong.

Pay careful attention to the cost of ownership for your dream rig. Older vans and trailers may need more frequent repairs and upgrades. And even the most expensive coaches have components that break, or require costly service by specialized technicians. How many of those repairs can you do yourself? Which ones will you need to outsource?

Before buying your first rig, reach out to owners of the same model. You'll find them in RV discussion forums and Facebook groups. Find out what they pay to maintain their rigs. Then consider how you'll deal with upkeep costs for the model you want.

In our opinion, towable RVs (trailers and fifth wheels) are the most affordable and smartest way to go when you start full-timing. Why? Because motorhomes are more expensive to own. If you purchase a motorhome and toad (towed car), you deal with the cost of maintaining and insuring *two* vehicles. You have two engines to maintain, two sets of wheels, etc.. Upkeep on two separate vehicles in addition to a motorhome's mechanical and house systems (plumbing, electrical, etc.) can be a pain. With a travel trailer or fifth wheel, you have only one engine and one house system to maintain.

The size of your rig and its ability to keep you comfortable in all weather conditions will determine where you can go and what you can do in it. When you look at potential rigs for full-time RVing, ask yourself:

- Is there comfortable living and work space to accommodate your income-generating methods?
- Do you love going off-the-beaten path to escape civilization for long periods of time? Or do you prefer RV park accommodations with full-hookups?
- Are you only comfortable on a king-size bed? Or do you care if you can't stand up in the bedroom?
- Do you have kids and pets who require extra space? Where will they sleep?
- Is there enough room for any extra gear you can't live without, like sports equipment or craft supplies?
- Is it a "four season" RV with adequate insulation around tanks and plumbing?

Lastly, ignore the dumb advice to "Get your last RV first." Many RVers believe you should choose the best and biggest RV you want now, because most RVers eventually upgrade anyway. In actuality, you may quickly get in over your head with debt and maintenance costs. Smart RVers start small, affordably, and move up from there.

RV Loan Debt is dumb: Just Say No

Do you drool over shiny new RVs? We do too! But we learned debt is dumb when Dave Ramsey told us it's best to purchase depreciating assets with cash. We came back down when we heard this advice after considering a loan on our second rig. Ramsey does **not** recommend getting a mortgage on an RV because RVs are depreciating assets. The only debt that is relatively "good" debt, he says, is a stick house mortgage. Real estate values go up. RV values do not.

Rene heard this directly from Dave when she called in to ask him about RV loans on his popular radio talk show:

> *Trailers go down in value...Mobile homes go down in value...It's a large car that you sleep in...You don't want to finance things that cost you. You don't want to finance anything, but for sure you don't want to finance something that's going down (in value). That's the direction.*
> *[PS] I think what you're doing is cool...*
> –THE DAVE RAMSEY SHOW
> SEPTEMBER, 2012

If you can't afford to pay cash for your RV, move on to another one that you can afford. Or, don't buy it at all and save until you can pay cash.

It's hard to restrain yourself from paying with plastic, and it takes tons of discipline to save up for a roadworthy vehicle that you buy with cash. But aren't you looking for *freedom* when you travel? If so, having a credit card or loan payment hanging over your head won't feel like freedom if your income dries up. Your dream lifestyle may quickly turn into a nightmare if you start it off in debt.

Debt is Dumb. Just say no. Carrying credit card debt is also dumb – even if you pay it off each month. We used to think we were debt-free because we paid our bills every month. We had one credit card for large routine expenses, like dental work and truck repairs which we always paid off each month, even if we had to dig from savings.

But there's a big problem with using credit cards this way. First, we weren't budgeting and saving our monthly income. When big expenses occurred, we just reached for the card. Using plastic gave us "Reward" points. It seemed to make sense until we realized we were riding "The Credit Card Float." It was a concept we never considered until Rene discovered the personal finance book, app and community known as "YNAB" – **You Need A Budget**.

> *Here's the test to determine if you are trapped in the float:* ==*If you can't pay the credit card in full right now AND meet your current obligations, you've got debt.*==
> –JESSEE MECHAM, YOU NEED A BUDGET

YNAB helped us realize that if we lost income, ==trying to pay all our monthly obligations and a card balance would instantly drain our savings==. So we stopped using the credit card.

Budget the Easy Way (with YNAB!)

Staying debt-free is an ongoing process. We stay on track by reviewing our financial situation almost every day with <u>YNAB: You Need a Budget</u>. This desktop and mobile app enables us to create a plan for every dollar we earn. With its global support network of free webinars and community discussions, we save more and have a better grasp on our money than ever before.

If you've never heard of YNAB, get acquainted by reading the book, "<u>You Need a Budget: The Proven System for Breaking the Paycheck-to-Paycheck Cycle, Getting Out of Debt, and Living the Life You Want</u>." Using their methods and app, you can keep track of spending and ultimately live more comfortably within your means.

We've tried many personal finance tools out there, from Dave Ramsey and David Bach to Suze Orman. They have all taught us plenty of tips and tricks for manging our finances. But none have had the positive, profound effect on our money habits the way YNAB has.

Three Reasons to Use YNAB Personal Finance Methods:
1. You won't feel broke or deprived on the YNAB system.
2. Your spending priorities aren't judged.
3. You'll build a solid financial future within a flexible budget framework that allows for inevitable ups and downs.

Founded in 2004 by accounting geek Jesse Mecham, the YNAB software for desktop and mobile device helps people reach financial success through four simple budgeting rules. It's not just for accounting geeks. Short, concise and useful, the <u>You Need a Budget</u> book helps you gain a better grasp on financial freedom.

Follow YNAB's Four Simple Rules:

Rule 1: Give Every Dollar a Job

For every dollar you earn, ask yourself: "What do I want this money to do for me?" When you make a plan for how and when to use every cent of your money, you get closer to your ultimate dream life. From rent to recreation, each month your task is to map out all spending priorities before money leaves your hand, just as you might plan your next road trip. If your spending priority means a double Frappucino every day at work, that's fine. Just be sure you can pay for it and still fund your other priorities within your current income level.

Rule 2: Embrace Your True Expenses

We all have them. Bills that go beyond the day-to-day costs of living like rent, fuel, and groceries are inevitable. These high dollar expenses can run us off the road if we're unprepared – like semi-annual insurance payments, personal income tax owed, and unexpected veterinary bills. The YNAB book teaches us to prepare for these inevitable financial hits by creating budget categories that encourage incremental funding for them throughout the year.

Rule 3: Roll with the Punches

This rule sets YNAB apart from all the other financial gurus who insist that if we stray from our budget we are financial losers. Instead, YNAB Rule Three teaches that a good budget is fluid enough to flow with inevitable life changes and spending priorities. For example, if you're short on money for food but have loads saved up for your vacation fund, just take it from that category, and make it a goal to replace that vacation fund draw next month. Stay accountable to the budget's bottom line (the amount of money coming in each month), and you'll slay it!

> *You're not accountable to every line item in your budget. That would be like holding yourself to that hour-by-hour schedule you wrote a week ago. It just won't match reality. But you are accountable to your bottom line – that is, the distance between your money in versus money out...*
>
> *That big picture thinking will keep you budgeting and moving closer to your goals...the goals are what matter. As long as you keep moving toward them, you're succeeding.*
> – YOU NEED A BUDGET

Rule 4: Age Your Money

Money goes in and money goes out. The longer money stays in your possession, the more peace of mind you attain. Rule Four shows how to build a reserve fund that breaks the paycheck-to-paycheck cycle. To do this, you'll build a pile of "old money" that stays in the bank for at least 30 days. The older the money, the more cash reserves on hand that allow you to cover regular *and* unexpected expenses.

> *Put another way: Without Rule Four, you've got a stack of bills waiting for money. With Rule Four, you've got a stack of money waiting for bills.*
> – YNAB

Get a firm grasp on your financial situation, and maintain a budget that meets all your needs. Budget for the long term and you'll finally experience true personal freedom! That's what we do, and it's how we keep our wheels turning for 15 years and counting.

Staying out of debt and following YNAB's rules give you a better idea of what you can afford as a full-time RVer, vandweller, or solopreneur. Put that knowledge to use, and you'll be on a path toward your dream life before you know it.

==The bottom line is this: If you want to live on the road, make it a priority to **earn more than you spend** and save for emergencies.==

> **Debt is not a tool**; *it is a method to make banks wealthy, not you. The borrower truly is slave to the lender.*
> — DAVE RAMSEY

Factor Connectivity Into Your Budget

Reliable internet access is a must if you plan to work from home wherever you roam. You cannot rely only upon RV park wifi if you intend to make a living online. We installed a satellite internet dish (and solar power) on our first rig because we knew we'd enjoy [boondocking](#) way off the grid. We soon learned that redundancy is the only true solution for getting online anytime, anywhere.

Our mobile mobile internet arsenal now includes multiple cellular broadband devices with different service providers, a [weBoost](#) cell signal booster, [satellite internet](#), and wired access if available for long term stays. Be sure to budget for the connectivity you will need to meet your specific internet usage demands. Learn more in our blog post: [Comparing Our RV Internet Options](#).

Throughout the rest of this book, we focus on the income side of things. We share what has worked for us, and present various other methods we've discovered to earn an Income Anywhere!

To access [highlighted links](#) throughout this book, save 50% OFF the e-book with coupon code: PAPERBACK Only at: https://liveworkdream.com/shop

RECOMMENDED READING

Nomadland
https://amzn.to/3JRvIA6

The Nomadland Myth
https://liveworkdream.com/2021/03/03/nomadland-real/

Rene Talks with Dave Ramsey
http://www.liveworkdream.com/2012/09/10/dave-ramsey-says-full-time-rvers-are-cool-rv-loans-arent/

The Total Money Makeover
https://amzn.to/3E850u3

You Need a Budget
https://amzn.to/3Gc9jWy

Our YNAB Book and App Review
https://liveworkdream.com/2017/12/27/book-for-full-time-rving/

Comparing Our RV Internet Options
https://bit.ly/rvinternetoptions

Mobile Internet Resource Center
https://www.rvmobileinternet.com/

The Authors with Financial Guru Dave Ramsey

HITTING THE ROAD

> **Workamping**
>
> FROM WIKIPEDIA, THE FREE ENCYCLOPEDIA
> HTTPS://EN.WIKIPEDIA.ORG/WIKI/WORKAMPING
>
> In the United States, "Workamping" is a [combination] of work and camping. A Workamper combines part-time or full-time paid or volunteer work with RV or tent camping. Workampers generally receive compensation in the form of a free campsite, usually with free utilities and additional wages. Workamping positions can include working at campgrounds, RV resorts, mobile home communities, Christmas tree or pumpkin sales lots, amusement parks, motels/hotels, national parks, state parks, U.S. Army Corps of Engineer locations, national monuments, lighthouses, retail stores, food service, sales and more. Workamping is particularly popular among retirees. While year round Workamping jobs do exist, many Workamping positions are seasonal.*

Rene Workamping at Vickers Ranch.

*While the definition of workamping has evolved over the years to encompass any type of work done while camping, we discuss this classic definition of the traditional workamper arrangement throughout this next section.

liveworkdream.com

WORKAMPING

How to Support Your Lifestyle with Workamping

Workamping is NOT a Career. But it can help you save money, explore new places, and have fun doing it.

We never thought it was possible to pay for long-term travel without eating up savings or going into debt. How did people afford to live on the road? What did they know what we didn't? Eventually, we discovered the secret to supporting the nomadic lifestyle: Workamping.

We were just a few months into our road trip when we set up camp in a remote national forest campground near Steamboat Springs, Colorado. There we met a clip-board carrying couple looking quite official as they checked things off a roster of campsites. We asked, "Are you the campground hosts?" Of course they were, and they explained to us the ins and outs of this thing called "workamping."

Jim and Mary were college professors on summer break. "We work here!" They proudly explained. No, they weren't getting paid "real money." But in exchange for just an hour or so of tidying up the campground each day, they got free rent for the season, a weekly honey wagon dump of their wastewater, fresh water delivery, and a small monthly stipend for incidentals like propane.

Work for poverty wages? It seemed like a crazy idea.

But Jim and Mary looked happy, and to us, the concept of trading some easy labor for a place to camp made total sense. Soon we started doing the same, and over the past fifteen years, workamping has been one part of our strategy that helps us stay on the road. It has both saved us money on rent and often provided extra cash. Workamping helps thousands of other full-time RVers like us keep costs down and hit the road before retirement age.

What is Workamping?

The traditional description of "Workamping" is a term originally coined by Workamper News, the first organization to connect RVers with RV parks and other employers offering part-time jobs or seasonal gigs. It's been going on longer than many RVers have been alive, and has evolved over the years. The traditional workamping arrangement typically involves temporarily working a given number of hours at a resort, public park, or tourist destination. In exchange, RVers receive free or discounted parking, often with perks like free use of guest amenities, no-cost laundry and propane.

Lately, workamping has evolved into a much larger scope of work opportunities. You'll find RVers doing warehouse work, farm harvests, and even clocking in as remote W2 employees. The original industry publication <u>Workamper News</u> has even revised their definition of workamping to include anyone who works while also camping. For this section we'll focus on traditional workamping. In the next sections we discuss being a remote employee, gig worker, or location independent entrepreneur.

Workamping Opportunities are Endless

Today's traditional workamping arrangements are both paid and unpaid, in the commercial, non-profit, and government sectors. Every industry is represented, from animal rescues to Amazon (see examples below). There seems to be no end to the kinds of arrangements available to help lower the costs of living when you're on the road. Workamping is a great way to explore new locations while saving on rent. Here's a general overview:

▶ Most employers seek to hire couples since only one campsite will be required for two workers. But many jobs are also available for solo workampers.

- Short term gigs exist, but they're harder to find since most employers don't want to retrain people every few weeks.
- Occasionally, workamping jobs offer housing or allow vans and tenting travelers, but these gigs are rare. Most employers require a self-contained RV in good condition.
- Some jobs offer pay. But many do not, and only offer a site in exchange for hours worked. Keep reading to learn about paid vs. volunteer workamping, and how to determine what is a "fair" trade.
- If your job works out, the business owner will often ask you to return next season.

Workamping can be an ideal situation if you're looking for somewhere to explore for a few months. And if you want to relocate or settle down somewhere, seasonal workamping helps build connections. You'll meet locals who can give you insight on an area that interests you for long-term living. Workampers tend to be a tight-knit group. ==Take a job to connect with like-minded nomads and build friendships on the road.==

What workamping is NOT

Even before the movie Nomadland was released, many full-timers were under the impression that workamping can take the place of a traditional job. Sorry, but we think they're wrong.

- Workamping Is NOT a long-term career strategy.
- Workamping will not replace the steady income of a "real" job or running your own business.
- Workamping won't help you become more marketable in "the real world."
- And if you want a more secure financial future, workamping won't do that either.
- Finally, If you go from one workamping gig to the

next, you'll never experience the type of connections and personal satisfaction gained from building a trade, or small business.

==Relying on workamping jobs as a primary income source is a bad idea.== Only a limited number of jobs offer living-wage salaries and benefits. Those that do are usually full-time positions that require related experience. Those jobs also require candidates to stick around for a year or longer, ruling out any possibility of long-term travel.

With workamping, you will very rarely find ways to advance your "career" and make more money. Workamper tasks like cleaning toilets, maintaining lawns, and answering phones are common. Over time if you gain enough workamping experience, you might get to work your way up to office or facilities management. But don't bet on it. Higher paying positions are usually filled by full-time employees, or returning long-term workampers.

Workamping is more of a means to an end, and a way to have fun doing it. It helps lower your cost of living while you craft a more fulfilling, long-term plan to support your way of life. Workamping can help you learn new skills and provide time needed to boost your own employment or business endeavors, or just enjoy your retirement years.

Treat workamping as one tool in your box of tricks that helps offset expenses. Focus on building alternative income streams we discuss in detail later, and keep growing those. Don't view workamping as a long-term career or you could be in for a huge disappointment.

What Kinds of Workamping Jobs Exist?

Workamping jobs run the gamut from RV resort maintenance and campground hosts, to seasonal warehouse workers or property caretakers for private homeowners. The vast majority of job duties aren't exactly rocket science. But many do involve physical labor that require workampers to be in good shape.

Workamping doesn't always mean answering phones or guiding guests to their RV sites either. Over the past 15 years, we have enjoyed various workamping jobs, yet never once had the stereotypical campground host or RV park worker gig. Some of the favorites we list on our <u>Live Work Dream Workamping Page</u> have been working on a ranch, hot springs resort, organic farm, and animal rescue.

Here are just a few fun jobs that may or may not pay a salary but are always far more interesting than cleaning toilets:

- Alaska Hospitality Worker
- Amazon Camperforce Warehouse Team Member
- JC Penney Distribution Centers
- DIGI-Key Fulfillment Center
- Animal Rescue Volunteer
- Campground Map Advertising Sales
- Circus / Fair employee (Midway staff)
- Fish Cannery Worker
- Fish hatchery volunteer (tagging fish and cleaning the facility)
- In-store demonstrator (cookware or utensil sales)
- Museum, Naturalist Docent
- National or State Park concession employee
- National or State Park campground host
- Natural Gas Line Surveyor
- Organic Farm Assistant (working farmer's market, harvesting produce and helping on the farm)
- Oil field gatekeeper (admitting workers into remote oil drilling sites)
- Park ranger assistant
- Property caretaker
- Ranch Hand
- RV park recreation leader

- Resort help (waitress, chef, housekeeper, store clerk, tour guide, ranch hand, etc)
- RV Park Maintenance/Clerk
- RV Technician
- Seasonal vendor (selling fireworks, pumpkins and Christmas trees)
- Sugar Beet Harvest Worker
- Theme Park Worker

Most traditional RV park and campground jobs don't pay, and usually require minimal hours. But many more employers are starting to pay workampers for every hour worked. For example, gate guarding for the oil industry can pay up to hundreds of dollars a day, in remote dusty locations demanding 24/7 on call duties. Fall and Winter also open up loads of paid seasonal workamping opportunities. It's one of the best times to try on the workamping lifestyle through short-term gigs. Opportunities include things like managing a Halloween store, selling pumpkins and Christmas trees. Many workampers follow agricultural harvests in the fall. Some earn a few thousand dollars working the sugar beet harvest in the Midwest. It's cold, hard, dirty work but it only lasts a few weeks and the money is great. Other workampers will pick apples at Pacific Northwest orchards. There is money to be made, for those willing to put in the work.

As seen in the movie Nomadland, many workampers become temporary Amazon employees to fill warehouse fulfillment jobs during the holiday crush. (Read about Rene's Amazon Camperforce experience to determine if this type of work might be for you!) JC Penney Logistics has implemented a Camp Crew Program. And Digikey is another major employer now integrating workampers into their distribution centers through their DIGI-KAMP Program.

Short-term jobs that enable you to earn a lot of cash

quickly often require working long hours in physically challenging roles. If you can survive the season you may make a few thousand dollars quite fast – as long as the harvest is good or holiday sales are robust.

To find all sorts of workamping jobs everywhere, read on for many helpful resources. And check the Files tab on the <u>Workampers Facebook Group</u> for more helpful links.

Our First Steps to Workamping

Once we agreed to try workamping, we decided that it would be a great way to get our hands dirty in work we had always been curious about. For instance:

- We <u>volunteered at an animal rescue</u> to find out if we were cut out to start our own dog rescue. It didn't take long to decide we weren't.
- The two of us <u>worked on an organic farm</u> to learn the ins and outs of farming. At the end of the season, we dropped our dream to start a farm.
- We <u>helped out at a hot springs resort</u> and worked as a "special team" renovating an RV park to see if we might become resort owners some day. Nope!

We were once caretakers at a property along the Mexican border. But our most favorite gig of all time has been <u>workamping job at Vickers Ranch</u>. This paying job has taught us many skills, and opened our eyes to running a ranch and hospitality business. It's fulfilling work, but we wouldn't want to bank our future on it. We returned to the Vickers for more than ten seasons, and still do occasionally. We love the challenging hands-on work, making new friends, living in gorgeous scenery, earning good pay, and creating fun memories.

Workamping has swayed us away from settling down and launching any sort of similar ventures. But it's also taught us that working online from our own home is the best sort of workamping for us.

Discovering Workamping Alternative Currency

Many workamping jobs offer what we call "alternative currency." This means that while you might not receive monetary compensation for a certain part of your job, you still get "paid" in various other ways. Freebies like no-cost laundry, propane, use of guest amenities, and sometimes free meals aren't uncommon. For example, when we worked on a farm we enjoyed free fresh organic vegetables and hands-on lessons for making our own biodiesel. At the hot springs resort we could soak for free in private tubs along the Rio Grande that cost guests $90+ an hour. While working on the ranch, we enjoyed many group meals and plenty of free laundry.

A handful of RV parks will pay for all hours worked, and then charge employees something for rent and electricity. Many KOA resorts are known to do this. But when they do it's usually at discounted rates.

Alternative currency bonuses are fun and can lower your cost of living for the short-term. But don't bank on them as an income source if financial security is your goal.

What is a "Fair Deal" in Workamping?

There is growing concern by some workampers that employers view workamping as a "free" source of labor. When looking at job postings on social media, these workampers "do the math" by strictly comparing hours worked and prevailing wages to rental rates at the park offering the job. If these workampers believe the employer isn't paying a fair wage – with site rent and/or paid hours – they publicly trash the business. We feel this is an unfair way to gauge fair pay, and like comparing apples to oranges.

These workampers usually fail to factor in the alternative currency that comes with the job, like free laundry and other amenities. They also don't consider a person's desire to be in a certain location, or learn a given skill. Everyone's definition of "a fair deal" is different. If working where you want to be is worth it to you for the pay and required hours, then that's a fair deal.

If it doesn't sound fair to you, then move on. There are plenty of other workamping jobs.

> NOTE: See our section about Workamping Pay (page 69) for a simple wage calculation chart to determine if a job offer is right for you.

Workamping Disadvantages

Workamping isn't always such a wonderful experience. You won't always have the same quality of accommodations as paying guests. Many of our workamping campsites have been nothing more than a spot in an open field, next to a barn, or in an ugly gravel lot. We've camped in a muddy field behind a barn with biodiesel runoff, horse poop flies and fire ant colonies all around us. At the time we wondered if we were insane to take that job. But we stuck it out, and are so glad we did! The experience of working on a small organic farm was priceless. We ate well, and in the end it convinced us that we were not cut out for the farming life.

Workamping is also like any workplace. At times it may feel like more of a job than a good time. You never know who you may be working with. Some workampers may be grumpy, or you might consider them nutbags. They may be smokers, might not share your views, or simply not be your kind of RVers. As for employers, some are easygoing folks you'll create lifelong friendships with. Others may be the kind of people you won't go out of our way to see again. If you fall into a job like that, do everyone a favor: be open and honest if you're not happy. And if you want to leave, give enough notice and an explanation.

How to Find Workamping Jobs on the Road

Workamping can seem mysterious at first, but thankfully there are many resources that help show RVers the ropes.

Join nomadic Facebook groups, like Workampers and Workamping in the USA. Such groups are filled with members willing to share their experiences. You'll find employer reviews, tips and advice, and job referrals.

Find workamping jobs and resources through Workamper News. This is the original membership-based organization that helps RVers find jobs around North America. Since 1987, they have published workamping jobs and resources via their Workamper News magazine, website (workamper.com), daily jobs hotline emails, classified listings, online seminars, and annual events.

As the oldest and largest organization focused on working from the road, Workamper News has helped us get hired at several workamping jobs that worked out great for us. By joining, you'll learn tips for creating workamping resumes and can even publish yours for employers to view on the Workamper website. Our "Awesome Applicant" resume has even landed us a few surprise job offers over the years.

Workamper News: Get details and promo code for premium membership at: https://bit.ly/wknpromo
---

Check out the popular Workers On Wheels website. Bob and Colleen at Work for RVers and Campers ran it for years, before she passed away in 2020. The site is still active and loaded with free job resources and workamping job opportunities. The archives include numerous helpful articles about legitimate work-from-home business ideas that can work for anyone living remotely. WOW shares paid employment and volunteer workamping opportunities and real-life examples of people living this fun lifestyle.

The site still offers numerous free resources about living and working remotely.

Escapees RVer Job Exchange is filled with remote work gigs. It's run by Xscapers, a community of Escapees RV Club, the largest and oldest RVers group in the world. The groups are an indispensable resource for anyone living and working from their RV. We recommend joining Escapees for their terrific RVers-only benefits ranging from mail forwarding to RV park discounts. While the majority of Escapees are retired folks, about twenty percent are working-age adults of all ages.

Caretaker Gazette is subscription-based, monthly newsletter. You'll find many property caretaking and house-sitting job classified ads, advice and information for property caretakers, house sitters, and landowners. Jobs are for locations all over the planet, so if you're interested in supporting an international travel lifestyle, this is a good place to begin. While the majority of positions are for long-term assignments (usually around 6 months or more), occasional seasonal positions are also listed.

Find many more helpful resources listed below. Numerous other websites and blogs maintain listings of traditional workamping jobs. But we have found none that compare to the amount, quality, and frequency of current jobs provided by the Workamper News website and daily Hotline emails. These often include listings from hospitality companies like Aramark and Xanterra that hire for many different service positions in various national parks, attractions, and other destinations.

Finally, most major RV resorts and RV park franchises have established workamper programs. Find workamping jobs around the country directly with companies like Kampgrounds of America (KOA), American Land and Leisure, or many others listed below.

POPULAR WORKAMPING RESOURCES
Workamper News
https://workamper.com/register-new-workamper
Use code AGRE6207 for any current promotions.

Workamping Jobs
https://workampingjobs.com/

Working Couples
https://workingcouples.com/

Happy Vagabonds
https://www.happyvagabonds.com/

Work for RVers and Campers
http://www.work-for-rvers-and-campers.com/index.html

Campground Maintenance Manager
https://campgroundmaintenancemanager.com

Kamper Jobs
https://kamperjobs.com/

VagaJobs
https://vagajobs.com/

LEADING RESORT CHAINS/FRANCHISES
Sun RV Resorts
https://careers.suncommunities.com/SunRVResorts/content/WorkCampers/

KOA Work Kamper Jobs
https://workatkoa.com/

Cal Am Resorts
https://www.cal-am.com/careers/

American Land and Leisure
http://www.americanll.com/employment

Recreation Resource Management – Camp Host Jobs
https://www.camphost.org/

American Land And Leisure Job Openings
http://www.americanll.com/Current_Openings.html

Great Escapes RV Resorts
https://www.greatescapesrvresorts.com/careers/

Equity Lifestyle Properties
https://www.equitylifestyleproperties.com/career-opportunities

DESTINATION HOSPITALITY EMPLOYERS

Westrek Services
https://www.westrekservices.com/

Aramark
https://careers.aramark.com/

Xanterra
https://www.xanterrajobs.com/

Vista Recreation
https://camprrm.com/jobs/
(Formerly Recreation Resource Management & California Land Management.)

Recreation Resource Management of America
https://rrmofa.com

Ortega National Parks
https://ortegaparks.com/

Audi Campground Services
https://www.audicampgrounds.com/

FEDERAL & STATE PARK SERVICES

US Army Corps of Engineers Campground Jobs
https://usace.usajobs.gov/

National Park Service Jobs
https://www.nps.gov/getinvolved
(Also search individual State Park sites for jobs.)

Yellowstone Jobs
https://www.nps.gov/yell/getinvolved/workwithus.htm
(Housing available for some positions.)

US Forest Service Jobs
https://www.fs.usda.gov/working-with-us/jobs

USA Jobs
https://www.usajobs.gov/

WAREHOUSE JOBS

Amazon Camperforce
https://amazon.com/camperforce

Digi-Kamp (Digikey Warehouse Jobs)
https://www.theunbeetableexperience.com/dk/

JC Penney Camp Crew Program
https://jcpwk.business.blog/

Rene's Amazon Experience Articles
https://liveworkdream.com/tag/rantazon

MISCELLANEOUS WORKAMPING RESOURCES

Alaska Tour Jobs
https://www.alaskatourjobs.com/

Alaska Excursions
https://www.alaskaexcursions.com/employment/

Work at Wall Drug
https://www.walldrug.com/about-us/employment

NOMADS Mission Volunteers
http://www.nomadsumc.org/
(Nomads On a Mission Active in Divine Service)

Federal Emergency Management Agency Jobs
http://www.fema.gov/careers

SEARCH FOR MORE WORKAMPING JOBS

RV Park Help Wanted Ads
http://www.rvparkstore.com/rv_park_help_wanted.htm

Indeed.com Campground Job Search Results
http://www.indeed.com/jobs?q=Campground

CoolWorks: Jobs with RV Spaces
http://www.coolworks.com/jobs-with-rv-spaces

Note: Join the Workampers Facebook Group for more workamping job search tips and to connect with fellow workampers!

Theme Park Workamping

Dollywood, Six Flags Darien Lake, and Adventure Land are a few attractions with established workamper programs. Search for amusement parks, living history museums, and other attractions near you to find more.

Dollywood
https://www.dollywood.com/Jobs

Six Flags Darien Lake
https://www.sixflags.com/darienlake/jobs

Adventure Land
https://www.adventurelandresort.com/employment/workamper

Silver Dollar City - Branson, MO
https://www.silverdollarcity.com

The Island in Pigeon Forge
http://www.islandinpigeonforge.com

Ranch and Farm Workamping Jobs

Our first long-term workamping gig was on an organic farm in Florida. (See all our posts about workamping at White Rabbit.) We've returned to our favorite ranch job for 10 years, and counting. (See all our posts about Vickers Ranch.) We found both jobs – and seen many other ranch and farm jobs – with our Workamper News subscription.

Ranch work isn't easy. Many of these jobs require experience, and all demand some strength, durability, and a certain amount of physical endurance. Don't expect to work with horses or livestock if you lack serious experience. Some may offer housing, and most are equipped to accommodate an RV. But you won't get a fancy site or frills and amenities. Some daily ranch duties are unpredictable as Colorado weather in summer. Certain farm jobs require doing the same backbreaking work every day, for little pay. The majority of ranch and farm work are full-time jobs. And most will not welcome minors or children.

The rewards of ranch workamping are wonderful though. That is, if you enjoy putting in a hard days work, often on your own in the middle of nowhere. You'll make friends with some of the most genuine people on earth by working closely with farmers and ranchers.

Search hard enough using the resources below, and you may find that perfect ranch job that meets your needs and fits your schedule. Play your cards right, and they might invite you back.

FARM & RANCH WORKAMPING RESOURCES

Farm and Ranch Jobs
https://www.farmandranchjobs.com/

WWOOF (World Wide Opportunities on Organic Farms)
https://wwoof.net/

EcoFarm
https://eco-farm.org/jobs

Cool Works
https://www.coolworks.com/ranch-jobs

Ranch World Ads: Ranch Jobs
http://www.ranchworldads.com/index.php?cat_id=4

Ag Hires
https://aghires.com/

RanchWork.com
https://www.ranchwork.com/

Farm Job List
https://farmjoblist.com/

Colorado Dude Ranch Jobs
https://www.coloradoranch.com/about-us/ranch-jobs/

Jooble
https://jooble.org/jobs-cattle-ranch

Simply Hired
https://www.simplyhired.com/
(Search "Farm and Ranch" in your desired state.)

Outdoor Workamping Jobs

Outdoor Industry Jobs
https://www.outdoorindustryjobs.com/

Indeed: Outdoor Jobs
https://www.indeed.com/q-Outdoor-jobs.html

Guide Jobs and Trip Leaders
https://www.coolworks.com/guide-jobs

Outdoor Adventures
https://www.coolworks.com/outdoor-adventures

Work in the Cannabis Industry

Having spent 10+ years in Humboldt county, we became familiar with the term "trimmigrants" long before the legal cannabis industry exploded. Now, any search for ranch and farm jobs will likely return seasonal work available for those interested in growing, trimming, grading, and packaging cannabis. You likely won't land a growing job without a Masters in Botany or Bioscience – or a proven track record and referrals. Come harvest time, however, thousands of jobs become available for trimmers and graders. And, with so many states legalizing cannabis, dispensaries are constantly hiring to fill retail and security jobs.

In addition to the few industry specific job portals we've found below, we also discovered that cannabis industry jobs are in all major job search engines. While few may offer traditional workamping arrangements, there is no shortage of jobs available for anyone wishing to work in the cannabis industry. Networking with legitimate cannabis business owners is another way to find your preferred position.

Cannacon is the major industry conference held at locations across the U.S throughout the year. During our last visit to Eureka, we wrote about our cannabis tourism research after attending the regional Cannifest.

Whether you want to work on a farm or as retail staff, a quick search can put you on the right path finding jobs as a trimmer, budtender, or security guard.

420-FRIENDLY RESOURCES AND RECOMMENDED READING
420 Careers
https://420careers.com/

Cannabis Jobs and Staffing
https://vangst.com/

Careers Cannabis
https://careerscannabis.com/

Cannabis Careers
https://www.marijuanajobscannabiscareers.com/

Hemp Staff
https://www.hempstaff.com/

Leafbuyer
https://jobs.leafbuyer.com/

WeedHire
http://weedhire.com/

How to Get Your Ideal Cannabis Farm Job
https://cannacon.org/cannabis-farm-job/

The Truth About Cannabis Tourism
https://liveworkdream.com/2017/05/10/cannabis-tourism/

"Offbeat" Workamping Opportunities

The circus and fair circuit is often hiring for everything from concessions and ride operators to set-up crew, drivers, and teachers. Want to join the circus? Check out our Workamper Expo Video from 2008. That first year on the road we attended the Florida expo and interviewed various employers hiring workampers for "unique" jobs. We discovered jobs for seasonal work at the Spirit Halloween store, nomadic product demonstrators, large RV resorts, amusement parks, and yes – the circus – among the many interesting opportunities for Workampers. And did we mention that was back in 2008?

Today there are even more offbeat workamping opportunities. Many state wildlife departments often hire workampers to check-in hunters for game seasons. Oil fields and other operations pay well for remote workamping security jobs. Southern Cross hires RVers as "mobile leak survey technicians' to inspect gas lines. And there are hundreds of circuses and carnivals on the road which always need help. If you can dream it up, add those keywords to "workamping" or "with RV site" to your next search.

WORKAMPING OUTSIDE THE BOX

Southern Cross Pipeline Inspection
https://www.southerncrossinc.com/

Sugar Beet Harvest Jobs
https://www.theunbeetableexperience.com/

Venardo Circus
https://www.venardoscircus.com/jobs

List of American Circuses
https://www.circusesandsideshows.com/circuses.html

Workaway – Cultural Exchange and Global Travel
https://www.workaway.info/

Circus Talk
https://circustalk.com/circus-jobs-and-circus-auditions

Carnival Jobs
https://carnivalwarehouse.com/marketplace/sort/employment

Spirit Halloween Store Jobs
https://www.spirithalloween.com/
http://www.work4spirit.com/

Work Exchange
https://www.helpx.net/

Caretaker Gazette
https://www.caretaker.org

Trusted Housesitters
https://www.trustedhousesitters.com/

Workamping As a Gate Guard

"Gate Guarding" is another workamping option for making up to a couple hundreds of dollars a day. Gate Guards must have a self contained RV, and most employers won't care about the age or condition. Usually only couples are hired, since this is usually a 24/7 on call job. You will likely park your RV in a very remote location with no services. A trailer with generator and water tank is usually provided, while dumping the tanks may have to wait for the weekly honey wagon visit. Your job may be boring at times, while you may also be rapidly checking numerous big rigs in and out from your location. That may be in the middle of the night, early morning, or Sunday afternoon. Someone must always be available, so don't plan on exploring the area together while workamping a gate job. We've heard horror stories about the smell, dust, snakes, and scorpions. But if you want or need to make $1050± per week, don't mind the accommodations, and can pass a background check, gate guarding may be for you.

Common gate guarding locations are found throughout the major oil and natural gas production regions. Gate jobs can also be found on wind and solar farms in the Southwest, and industrial or mining operations around the country. We've never personally done this, however, we have heard stories from others in the Facebook Workampers Group. Many bloggers sharing their experiences can also be found with a quick search.

GATE GUARD EMPLOYERS & RESOURCES:

Guardian Industries
https://guardian-industries.com/

Guard 1
http://www.guard1services.com

Spartan Protection Services
https://www.spartanprotectionservice.com/contract-opportunities

Timekeepers Inc.
https://Facebook.com/TimekeepersInc

S&S Gate Services
https://ssgateservices.com/

J & G Security
http://oilgates.com

Gate Guard Services
https://gateguardservices.com/

Primo Gate Guard Services
http://primogateguards.com/

OverWatch Gate Guard Services
http://www.overwatchent.com/

Video: Comprehensive Guide To Gate Guarding Part 1 of 3
https://youtu.be/_cJW4BQTy0A

More Tips to Find Your Ideal Workamping Job

Work with Like-minded People

If you seek workamping jobs at places that you enjoy visiting, you're more likely to encounter other like-minded folks. For example, we love soaking in hot springs, which tend to attract the type of bohemian spirit we enjoy. So when we took jobs at the laid-back hot springs resort in New Mexico, we found we shared a lot in common with guests, fellow workampers, and management. This made the experience memorable and enjoyable. Flexible hours and free soaks helped make up for the hard work too!

Know Your Time Limitations

Stick to your priorities before accepting an offer. If you can only work a few hours a week because of other commitments, don't take a job that requires you to do more. Working additional non-paid hours in lieu of your "real" work will set you on the road to resentment faster than you can say, "I quit." When interviewing with employers, make it clear that you can give 110% when on duty, but you have other responsibilities. Let them know if you can't give more hours than the advertisement described.

Know your Physical Limitations

Don't take a job if you have any doubts about performing certain physical tasks. For example, some Amazon workampers must be capable of standing on their feet for up to 12 hours daily and may not sit on a chair except during breaks. Warehouse and harvest job requirements also often required the ability to lift at least 50 pounds, sometimes many times a day.

We know of some workampers who took such jobs anyway. These folks quit within a few weeks when strain or exhaustion set in. Social and emotional limitations are other concerns to consider when taking a job that entails customer contact. If you have a disorder causing stress when engaging with strangers, or are shy and hesitant to meet new people, don't take a job that requires you to work with the public.

Always ask the employer to describe every job duty in detail. For example:

- Can I sit while working? How long will I have to stand on my feet?
- Will I be asked to lift heavy objects, bend over regularly or climb ladders? If so, will I work in teams?
- What is the work environment like? For example, will I work outdoors during any weather or inside an air-conditioned office?
- What kind of people skills are you looking for?

Know What You're Getting Into

How do you know if workamping is right for you? When you talk to an employer about a seasonal job, you'll want to ask as many questions about your role as if you were interviewing for a permanent position. Whether you're working four hours a week or forty, those hours can be miserable unless you are prepared for what may lay ahead.

When you work for smaller campgrounds or parks, job descriptions may not exist. These mom and pop businesses need workampers to be flexible and wear many hats. If you always worked for large organizations and prefer sticking to the predictability of a job with a strict description, look for larger corporate owned resorts with many workampers, detailed job descriptions, and departmental systems in place. Also consider opportunities at amusement parks, the U.S. Army Corps of Engineers (USACE) park system, and state or national parks.

Important things to consider with any job include:

- What are the general job duties, pay and any benefits?
- The amount of training and supervision provided to you.
- Your start and end date, how many hours you'll work and when your days off will occur.
- If your partner is working too, will s/he be able to have the same schedule and take the same days off?
- If you have children, are they welcome and will you have separate hours than your partner.
- Are your pets welcome, and are there any breed restrictions?
- What amenities or perks are available to workampers?
- What are the workamper accommodations like, and are there any restrictions on the RV types permitted?
- How far is it to the nearest fuel, groceries, pharmacy, veterinarian, or any other services you may need?

Take your own desires and needs into consideration too:

- How much do I like the company, the location, and my potential teammates?
- Am I comfortable with the job duties? Can I physically perform them?
- Considering all the perks, are the job requirements fair for the time I put in.
- Is there anything about this job that I might not like?

Note: See Appendix for More Questions to Ask Workamping Employers.

er Workamping Considerations

Why You Should Reach Beyond Your Comfort Zone

Sometimes pushing yourself beyond your comfort zone in a workamping job can pay off. Short-term gigs that you never would have considered in your previous life can open the door to great opportunities.

For example, we have enjoyed many workamping opportunities – both paid and unpaid. Each has had unique pros and cons, but always made our life more adventurous and fun. Once we applied for work as a paid ranch hand and housekeeper. The owner called us and during our conversation, we felt a little unsure about the work. Job descriptions were vague and he seemed surprised that we wanted him to sign a workamping agreement (he did sign and return it promptly, however). The only information we could find about the business and the area, was that it was located in an outdoor lover's paradise.

The job paid well, so we took it. On our journey to the ranch, we repeated the workamper's mantra: "If we don't like it, we can turn the key and leave!" But it didn't take long to know we made the right choice. The location was stunning. It was rustic, with trees, lakes and streams everywhere. The owner and his family were a welcoming bunch whose family homesteaded the area over 100 years ago. Most of their guests had been coming for generations. Obviously, it was a good place to be, and we are so glad we stuck it out. Despite the work being some of the most physically challenging we've ever done, it was an enjoyable experience. We've returned to Vickers Ranch almost every season since, and are always welcomed back like family.

Finally, if you have retired from a high-paying job or never had a "dirty job", don't rule out non-paying jobs and never put cleaning campsites or bathrooms beneath you. You might miss out on some of the best memories the workamping lifestyle offers.

liveworkdream.com

How to Mix Business and Workamping

Holding down a non-paid workamping job while being self-employed or working remotely can present a challenge. Many larger employers, like the National Park Service, often ask at least 20 hours a week for a campsite trade, leaving little time for workampers to do anything else. Retired people who don't need to focus on making money can choose from a larger selection of jobs than those of us who are still earning a living.

Don't worry if you can't find a workamping job with hours that accommodate your other money-making efforts. Those jobs are out there, you'll just need to look a little harder to find them. We once took a workamping job – without pay – that only required us to work 5 hours a week (each) as RV park maintenance staff. Other assignments have also enabled us to continue our regular online business activities. The time we <u>worked at the hot springs resort</u> was with a three days on / three days off schedule. Our caretaking gig in southern Arizona only required us to be there and periodically water trees, with a few hours put into a remodel project over the few weeks we were there.

Juggling a workamping job and having a small business is possible. You can make it work, just like we do. Focus on finding and keeping that favorite job with an employer who understands. Be firm in the hours you're willing to work. Your business comes first!

Keep <u>making connections</u>, talk to other workampers, and if you find a good job that seems like it will give you the right amount of free time, don't wait to apply. If you enjoy it and the hours are good, do everything possible to ensure you'll be hired again next season.

Workamping with Pets

If you have pets that need daily supervision, you'll want a workamping job that enables you to check on your ani-

during any long shifts. If you can't do it, who will be used to help? Ask if a local dog walker is available to assist. Many workampers are happy to swap dog walking duties with their teammates. Ask the employer if your dog is allowed on the job, or how you can work around your pet's needs.

Considerations about workamping with pets

- Will the boss allow me to check in on my pet throughout the day? Not just for lunch, but for pee breaks and walks?
- How close will I be workamping to my rig? Will I be so far away that I can't get there in time if necessary. Say for example, a bear tries to get inside? Yes, that really happened to us when Jerry was alive.
- Is the workamping location safe for my pet? For instance, is it so close to a highway that if my pet escaped they could get hit by a car? Do they have adequate outdoor play and potty spaces?
- What about other workampers and their pets? Are the campsites so close that our pets will be nose-to-nose? Are those other pets sociable? Will my animal constantly feel threatened, or act aggressively toward those pets?
- What about wild animals and livestock? Is my pet friendly toward other critters?
- Can I get my pet's food brand easily shipped to me? Or is there a good pet food store within driving distance?
- And what about veterinary care? Are there any vet clinics nearby? How far is it to the nearest emergency clinic?

Choosing a Workamping Location

Before you agree to any job, consider how far your workamping job site is from shopping and services. If it's in a rural area, ask yourself if you want to spend your only precious time off making the long haul to town. This was a challenge for us during our eat-local challenge while working at our favorite Rocky mountain ranch one summer!

We once met a campground host in Big Bend National Park – where there is no cell phone coverage and the nearest services are hours away. He reinforced this point when discussing senior workampers. "If you have physical challenges or ongoing medical needs," he said, "don't come somewhere like this."

Let's Talk About Workamping Pay

If your workamping job will be performed in exchange for a campsite at a for-profit company, Workamper News recommends the formula below to determine if it's an even trade.

Add the following:

+ Campsite value (monthly or seasonal rate)

+ Hookups / utilities

+ Perks (propane, laundry, meals, etc.)

+ Any wages / salary

Divide this total by # of hours worked each month

TOTAL = Equivalent Hourly Wage

According to Workamper News, most workamping jobs' hourly equivalent wage is somewhere between $7 and $15 per hour. When you consider the current federal minimum wage, its up to you whether or not you want to work for less. This is especially true if the employer will ask you to supervise others or utilize any special skills or training you already have (such as plumbing or accounting). Workamper recommends avoiding jobs that ask you to work more hours than a long-term customer would be charged in cash.

What about jobs that don't pay?

Workamper believes that in most situations, 15 hours per week is a fair trade for a full hookup campsite, whether that amount is shared between a couple or performed by a single person. However, you also need to consider if a job has special perks, like the free horseback rides we enjoyed while working at the dude ranch. These would have cost us $120 each as paying customers. Our access to free Jeep use on the ranch, or private soaking at the hot springs resort was worth hundreds of dollars. The value of these types of perks must also be taken into consideration.

Finally, there is one benefit of every workamping job which only you can assign a value. That is **your own personal desire** to be in a certain location, or perform certain tasks.

Perhaps the math for a particular job comes out to paying less than minimum wage. Or maybe the hours add up to be worth more than the going rate at the park. But maybe your campsite is in a beautiful location along a world-class fly fishing river, during the big steelhead run. Or, what if you're retired and all you have to do is drive the mini train around the resort, and you enjoy being around kids having fun? Is it worth it to put in a few extra hours to have free rent in Maine for prime leaf-peeping season?

These are those alternative forms of currency that add up to enjoying some of the best experiences the workamping lifestyle has to offer.

Do You Need to Get It in Writing?

So you found the perfect workamping job, and now it's time to make it official. The best employers will send you a written job description and employment agreement to sign. If they don't, Workamper News strongly suggests getting a signed contract from your employer. This provides an understanding of job requirements and reimbursement.

Ultimately, a workamper contract may not be worth the paper its printed on. Most formal workamping job agreements are "at will employment" arrangements. These allow either party to terminate the job for any reason without notice. Accountability of the contractees, however, may vary depending upon the state where you're working. In California for example, state employment laws often override any contractual agreements.

Many small parks or mom and pop employers may not care for the formality of a contract. You may be passing up a great opportunity by asking for one. On the other hand, we have heard plenty of nightmares from workampers who traveled thousands of miles, only to discover there was no job waiting for them. Perhaps the duties were nothing like what they discussed. Maybe the hiring manager was no longer there, or perhaps the park has changed ownership. These things happen.

The contract choice is a personal one. You'll need to make a judgment call based on the amount of risk you're willing to take when accepting the job.

If your employer doesn't have an agreement, ask if you can send one that describes everything you were told about the position. Check out the suggested Sample Work Agreement from Workamper News.

Once you agree to a position, stop looking!

Many workampers will accept several job offers then flake out on all but one when the time comes to roll into the park. If you found a job good enough to apply for and you got it, show up and find out if it's the right place for you. Your employer is counting on you to help them through the season. Honesty matters most and communication is key. Be upfront about any challenges you encounter on the job before they become major issues.

What About Taxes?

Confirm with any employer whether you will be considered a contractor or employee. You need to know before accepting the job if they'll be filing 1099 or W2 paperwork.

If you work in taxable income states, you'll need to file taxes in every state where you worked. In addition, some aspects of trading a campsite for work are also taxable, so consult with a certified tax expert to ensure you're filing proper paperwork. Ideally you'll want someone familiar with the full-timing lifestyle, and filing income tax in multiple states.

The popular book Can I Write Off My RV? What Every Rver Should Know About Taxes is an older resource now, but still very relative regarding the basics. Taxes for RV Owners 2019 Edition, is a more current book by an authorized tax advisor who promises to share, "what every full-time RVer should know about taxes."

The Workamper News Article Archives are another excellent resource for expert professional advice to help ensure you have no surprises come tax time. Access to these tools and more is another reason to consider a Premium Workamper Subscription with promo code AGRE6207.

Learn more about workamping and taxes:
https://xscapers.com/workamping-and-taxes/

Don't Like Your Job? Turn the Key and Leave

Workamping jobs should be treated with the same amount of respect as any other job you've held, even if you're not getting paid in cash. This goes for both workampers and employers. But if despite your best efforts to make the most of it, you find that it's not agreeing with your expectations, remember you always have the option to turn the key and leave.

Before you tell your boss to shove it, however, keep in mind that the workamping community is a small one and competition for the best jobs is tough. Positive referrals go a long way when applying for that perfect job. And your reputation could follow you to your next assignment. Also, workamping jobs are in especially short supply during winter months so try not to burn any bridges if you want year-round work.

If you need a workamping job to support your nomadic lifestyle, have something else lined up before leaving one and moving on to the next. Better yet, start developing additional income streams – which we get into in more detail next.

Still want to quit? Give your employer plenty of notice, provide a fair explanation, and try to leave with a good referral. Help the employer and future workampers by being honest and clearly communicating why the job isn't working out for you.

RECOMMENDED READING

Workamper News
https://workamper.com/register-new-workamper
The leading resource for finding workamping jobs, with daily listings, forums, online resume builder and more! New subscribers get any current promotion and free issue with promo code AGRE6207.

Workamping at Vickers Ranch
https://liveworkdream.com/tag/vickers-ranch

Read About All Our Workamping Experiences
https://liveworkdream.com/workamping

Live Camp Work: How to Make Money While Living in an RV and Travel Full-Time
https://amzn.to/3Bi7DHG

Live Camp Work: Working RVers Logbook & Workamping Jobs Tracker
https://amzn.to/3nvyjQo

Support Your RV Lifestyle: An Insider's Guide to Working on the Road
https://amzn.to/3Gpg1sC

WORKAMPING

So, You Want To Be A Workamper?
https://amzn.to/3mfwCad
Read our book review:
http://www.liveworkdream.com/2014/02/05/huggins-workamping-book-review/

Seasonal Workamping for a Living: How We Did It
https://amzn.to/3pERfyR

RV Living: A Complete Beginners Guide to a Budget Friendly RV Lifestyle and Workamping
https://amzn.to/3CkjqXs

Live Your RV Dreams: The Beginners Guide to Workamping
https://amzn.to/3bbMEMj

Work Your Way Across The USA: Travel And Earn A Living Too!
https://amzn.to/2XNaD14

Can I Write Off My RV?
https://amzn.to/3bcPQaa

Taxes for RV Owners 2019 Edition
https://amzn.to/3uUHBLi

Find more Workamping books on Amazon.
https://amzn.to/3nzitnQ

Jim workamping at Riverbend Hot Springs

ADDITIONAL WORKAMPING RESOURCES:

Workampers Facebook Group
http://www.Facebook.com/groups/weloveworkamping/

Live Work Dream: Workamping
https://liveworkdream.com/workamping

Live Work Dream Workamping Posts and Reviews
https://liveworkdream.com/tag/workamping

Gone Workamping
https://goneworkamping.com/

Live Camp Work
https://livecampwork.com/workampingjobs/

Wanderlust Estate
https://wanderlustestate.com/workamping/

Wander Jobs
https://wanderjobs.com/

My Adventure Jobs
https://myadventurejobs.com/

Cheap RV Living: Workamping
https://cheaprvliving.com/kb/workamping/

RV Forum: Workamping
https://www.rvforum.net/forums/workamping.53/

How NOT to Find a Workamping Job

The best way to secure a workamping job is to contact the employer directly. Pick up the phone. And call back if you do not get a response. If you simply comment on a Facebook post and wait, you'll likely be looked over for someone with more initiative.
From @LiveWorkDream: https://bit.ly/hownotgetjob

Another hard day at work. Near Moosehead Lake, Maine.

Do the one thing you think you cannot do. Fail at it. Try again. Do better the second time. The only people who never tumble are those who never mount the high wire. This is your moment. Own it.
– OPRAH WINFREY

Wealth is not his that has it, but his that enjoys it.
– BENJAMIN FRANKLIN

Fortune sides with him who dares.
– VIRGIL

MAKING MONEY

More Ways To Support Your Nomadic Lifestyle

Before the pandemic, the majority of full-time RVers that we knew were either living off their savings, retirement funds, or self-employed. The option to work remotely was a distant dream for most people living the default life. Then everything changed when COVID-19 forced businesses to send employees home to work.

Today, millions of people are happily working from wherever they park, and showing their employers that productivity doesn't need to happen in a cubicle. More tools than ever facilitate working from home. And there has never been more ways to earn a living on the road.

Is Remote Employment in Your Future?

A report from the popular talent marketplace Upwork titled, "<u>Future Workforce Report 2021</u>," revealed that 73% of managers see the value in remote work and hiring independent professionals. In fact, 48% of those hiring are currently working with contract talent.

Key Remote Work Employment Statistics in 2021

- 16% of companies in the world are 100% remote.
- 44% of companies don't allow working remotely.
- Better work-life balance is the main reason why people choose to work remotely.
- 77% of remote workers say they're more productive when working from home.
- The average annual income of remote workers is $4,000 higher than that of other workers.
- 85% of managers believe that having teams with remote workers will become the new norm.

- 74% of workers say that having the option to work remotely would make them less likely to leave a company.
- The three biggest challenges associated with remote work are unplugging after work (22%), loneliness (19%), and communication/collaboration (17%).

Let's begin with remote employment. Whether your current employer offers a remote work program, or you want to find one that does, this information should prove helpful. If you have an entrepreneurial spirit and are more inclined to go it on your own, you may consider skipping ahead to our sections about the Gig Economy and Starting Your Own Business.

Does your company allow remote work?

Working from home used to be a prize for the top ranks within a company. But the pandemic has opened the flood gates for almost all office workers to work remotely. If you don't yet have a remote work arrangement with your company, there's no better time to ask for one. We know full-time RVers who have managed to negotiate this arrangement with their employer. But we haven't had a "real job" since we became self-employed in 1998. So we can't tell you how to negotiate the best remote work arrangement. Here are some great articles that tell you how to do it far better than we can:

- CNBC: **How to negotiate a permanent work-from-home arrangement**
  If you find yourself in that camp but your employer has already announced plans to return to the office, or they haven't made a decision yet, experts tell CNBC Make It that now is a good time to try and make your situation permanent. Here's how to make the ask.

- FORBES: **How To Ask Your Boss To Work From Home Permanently**
If you want to continue working remotely but aren't sure how to approach the conversation with your boss, implement the suggestions in this article. The goal is to engage in a productive dialogue with your boss that supports your goal of a more permanent work-from-home arrangement while also expressing its immense benefits to your employer.
- TODAY: **How to ask your boss to work remotely full time**
If you count yourself among those advocating for remote work and could use some advice on how to approach the conversation, read this article for expert advice. Today asked several workplace authorities to share their tips to help you head into a discussion with confidence about continuing to work from home

---

To access highlighted links throughout this book, save 50% OFF the e-book with coupon code: PAPERBACK Only at: https://liveworkdream.com/shop

---

How to Find Remote Jobs

Is your employer opposed to you working remotely? Want a remote job that really rocks your world? Don't give up yet. Those jobs are out there. Start by searching the Internet to find work-from-home remote jobs using these search terms:

- "companies that hire remote workers"
- "jobs that allow you to work from anywhere"
- "jobs that can be done from anywhere"
- "jobs that can be done from home"
- "now hiring remote workers"
- "online jobs that can be done anywhere"
- "jobs you can work from home"

You may find your ideal remote job hiding in these search results. Below are job search portals and additional resources for finding remote employment, as well as a few companies smart enough to have a remote workforce.

REMOTE EMPLOYMENT RESOURCES

LinkedIn Jobs
https://www.linkedin.com/jobs/
If you're serious about finding a good paying professional job, you need to be on LinkedIn. Select "Remote" from the Jobs page to search thousands of opportunities.

Monster.com
https://www.monster.com/jobs/search?q=&where=remote
Search "remote" for thousands of jobs you can work from home.

Zip Recruiter
https://www.ziprecruiter.com/
Rated #1 Job Site in the U.S. (G2 Reviews, 2021)

Upward
https://www.upward.net/
Employers invite you to apply based on your profile

Remote.co
https://remote.co/
Exclusively remote jobs and resources.

Remotely Possible
https://www.remotelypossible.tech
Job board and resources for finding remote employment.

Career Builder
https://www.careerbuilder.com/
Search jobs by skills. View salaries. One-click apply.

Acquent
https://aquent.com/find-work/?k=remote
Find remote jobs perfectly matched to your unique talents.

SkillGigs
https://skillgigs.com/
A simple and easy portal for getting in front of employers hiring remote workers in medical, tech and administration.

Indeed.com
https://www.indeed.com/jobs?l=remote
Employment marketplace with 300,000+ remote job listings the last time we checked.

FlexJobs – Find a Better Way to Work
https://www.flexjobs.com
Find thousands of remote, hybrid, & flexible jobs.

Growmotely
https://www.growmotely.com/
Culture-matching skilled professionals, with growing companies offering long term remote jobs.

Otta
https://otta.com/
Job search engine with thousands of remote and flexible opportunities.

Liveops
https://www.liveops.com/
Virtual, flexible call center jobs

The Dots
https://the-dots.com/
The professional network for people who don't wear suits to work.

AngelList
https://angel.co/
Join the world's largest startup community.

WorkMarket
https://www.workmarket.com/
Download app for workers to access assignments.

Swipejobs (App)
https://www.swipejobs.com/
Swipejobs is the first app-based virtual staffing company available for iOS and Android.

POPULAR COMPANIES WITH REMOTE WORKFORCE

Thousands of companies hire remote employees. Here are just a few. Search for others by adding "remote" to your keywords.

AMAZON Remote Employment
https://www.amazon.jobs/en/search?base_query=remote
Amazon is offering teams more flexibility on where to work.

Automattic
https://automattic.com/work-with-us/
The creators of WordPress and WooCommerce are frequently hiring for their distributed workforce with hundreds of open positions across more than 70 countries.

Defiant
https://www.defiant.com/employment/
Defiant is a 100% remote security technology company, often hiring for development, quality assurance and customer service.

DropBox
https://www.dropbox.com
Join Dropbox and design your dream career from anywhere.

Belay
https://belaysolutions.com/
Virtual jobs for VAs, bookkeepers, web development, and social media experts.

Sutherland Global
https://jobs.sutherlandglobal.com/
Work on interesting projects with great people wherever you are.

Incsub
https://incsub.com/careers/
Melbourne based tech company always hiring remote employees for jobs from sales, marketing, and HR, to development and customer support.

Shopify
https://www.shopify.com/careers/
From websites to warehouses, there's a place for engineers and developers of all backgrounds at Shopify.

You Need A Budget
https://www.youneedabudget.com/careers/
YNAB produces a suite of popular budgeting apps, and has a 100% workforce with flexible hours.

REMOTE EMPLOYER LISTS

50 Virtual Companies that Hire for Work-From-Home Jobs
https://www.flexjobs.com/blog/post/25-virtual-companies-that-thrive-on-remote-work-v2/

30 Companies Switching to Long-Term Remote Work
https://www.flexjobs.com/blog/post/companies-switching-remote-work-long-term/

RECOMMENDED READING

Remote: Office Not Required
https://amzn.to/319YZ1F

Remote Work Revolution: Succeeding from Anywhere
https://amzn.to/3pN3olk

Find Your Happy at Work: 50 Ways to Get Unstuck, Move Past Boredom, and Discover Fulfillment
https://amzn.to/2XOI8jw

Great Pajama Jobs: Your Complete Guide to Working from Home
https://amzn.to/2ZtvS9f

How To Thrive In Remote Working Environments: Make Remote Work All It Should Be
https://amzn.to/31cNXsF

The Best Work-From-Home Jobs For 2020: 144 Legitimate Remote Jobs That Are (Almost) Always Hiring
https://amzn.to/2ZBKenJ

Great Jobs You Can Do From Home: How To Find Real Work-From-Home Jobs
https://amzn.to/3Gt2Wi9

WORK FROM HOME WHILE YOU ROAM: The Ultimate Guide to Jobs That Can Be Done From Anywhere
https://amzn.to/31cSM5f

WORK FROM HOME JOB IDEAS: A Genuine Collection of Verified Online Business Resources
https://amzn.to/3GrSO9i

WORK FROM HOME JOBS FOR MOMS: Passive Income Ideas for financial freedom life with your Family
https://amzn.to/3BmP31g

Stay at Home Jobs for Moms: An Essential Guide to Finding Work and Making Money from Home
https://amzn.to/3pRvVpM

Remote work is the future of work."
– ALEXIS OHANIAN, REDDIT

Remote Work That's Made for RVers

One category of remote employment of specific interest to RVers is campground map publishing. Every RVer has received a campground map from RV parks they've visited. These campground site maps include advertising for local businesses nearby. There are two leading companies that manage the production of these maps – AGS, and Southeast Publications (SEPI).

Both companies hire remote employees. And it is usually teams of RVing representatives and independent contractors who do the ad sales and production. These are often full-time jobs which allow RVers to enjoy their travels to each new RV park client. During their stay, they will sell advertising to local businesses and manage production of the park maps. When the project is done, they'll move on to the next park. We are good friends with a couple who made a lucrative living working as sales reps and regional managers for AGS Publications. Rene wrote in detail about Larry and Nancy's AGS career in her rvlife.com interview titled, <u>Finding the Right Job</u>.

RV Park photography and marketing is another remote job opportunity for RVers to consider. HipCamp is one website that actively recruits freelance photographers to gather photos of campgrounds and other outdoor destinations. National Airviews is an aerial photography company known to hire independent sales representatives throughout the mid-Atlantic region. Dronegenuity is another that hires independent drone pilots. A search for "rv park marketing" or "campground drone photography" will likely return more results.

RECOMMENDED READING
RV Life: AGS Reps Interview
https://rvlife.com/finding-the-right-job/

RVER REMOTE JOB RESOURCES

AGS Publications
https://www.agspub.com/
RV Park Map/Ad Sales and Production

Southeast Publications
https://southeastpublications.com/
RV Park Map/Ad Sales and Production

HipCamp
https://www.hipcamp.com/
Get paid to photograph and visit unique places.

National Airviews, Inc.
https://www.nationalairviews.us/
Aerial Photography Sales

Dronegenuity
https://www.dronegenuity.com/careers/
Drone Pilot Jobs

"Home-Based Business" Opportunities

Taking Baby Steps to Self-Employment with Network Marketing, Revenue Sharing & MLM

Let's say working remotely lights your fire, but you prefer the idea of being your own boss and making your own hours. Perhaps you're not keen on trying to start your own business from scratch. Or maybe you have no idea where to begin. Partnering with an established company as a remote marketing executive may be best for you. Many network marketing and multi-level marketing (MLM) companies have earned a bad reputation over the years – most with good reason. Yet there are countless people making serious money with legitimate niche product companies which have stood the test of time, or provide a fair and well-founded business model.

Franchise and revenue sharing business models are more popular than ever. When you partner with a company that already has an established product and distribution model, you cut out many of the steps to getting your own business off the ground. Partnering with companies like these are appealing to many people who are not ready or don't want to start a new business on their own.

> Do your research before you sign up with any network marketing or revenue sharing business!

Many MLMs deliver what they promise, but there are just as many that do not. While their organizational structure and profit distribution model may resemble a pyramid, they are not **all** "pyramid schemes".

Know what to look for when reviewing the business model and revenue distribution. Read on for tips to weed out the scams and schemes from legitimate opportunities with serious potential.

The world is full of unethical network marketing companies and fly-by-night operations promising big financial profits in exchange for little effort. Lots of people get burned by phony schemes that promise easy money while working from home. If you're considering these types of work-at-home opportunities, always investigate the company, its products and the compensation plan before getting involved.

You must believe in the product

Never jump on board just for the promise of income potential. If you don't personally use and enjoy the product(s), you will never be able to reliably represent the company. And people will see right through any marketing message you deliver.

Watch Out for Scams!

Maybe you've already investigated home-based business opportunities, and perhaps they seemed promising at first. But how many turned out to be a waste of time, money and effort? We know how easy it might sound to get sucked into a promising "make money at home" scheme.

It is likely a Network Marketing Scheme if:

- You have been offered a chance to "Get in on the ground floor" or join a program or where you must recruit new members to make money.
- The "business" involves no actual goods or only services of little or no value that just serve to promote the opportunity (such as training materials).
- You are expected to "invest" in huge up-front costs to pay for large quantities of goods.
- You are required to stock up monthly on inventory items you could never use yourself.

Many MLM programs and pyramid schemes try to disguise themselves as a legitimate revenue sharing business. You can ask yourself two questions to recognize these scams:

1. Do you earn financial rewards based on actual product sales, either by yourself or others you have introduced to the program?
2. Are the products you represent genuine items of real value, sold at a reasonable price to consumers who will want to purchase them again?

Answering no to either of these questions should be a big red flag that you are dealing with a scammy MLM program or pyramid scheme.

NOTE: If you're already a skeptic, but considering a great sounding opportunity, check out these sites:

- **MLM Watch**
  https://quackwatch.org/mlm/
  The Skeptical Guide to Multilevel Marketing
- **Multilevel Marketing (MLM) vs. Pyramid Scheme – Red Flags to Watch For**
  https://www.moneycrashers.com/multi-level-marketing-mlm/
  An Overview and Red Flags to Watch For

▶ **The Anti-MLM Coalition**
https://mlmtruth.org/
Anti-MLM writers providing support & advice for anyone affected by this industry.

Multi-Level Marketing: What Works, What Doesn't

Multi-level marketing businesses aren't all bad. Dozens of companies have existed for a long time and they've helped many enthusiastic marketers generate healthy incomes. Many network marketing and direct selling businesses are out there recruiting folks who want to start a home-based business. They usually promise big profits and quick start up, without any hassle or risk. But we would never risk our reputation, and personal finances, on any traditional MLM business. For the vast majority of serious entrepreneurs, this business model simply does not work.

Most MLM businesses only work if there is an endless supply of new associates joining on a regular basis. But in reality, the attrition rate tends to be high. The number of people being recruited – and the amount of new money they bring in – tends to dry up quickly. In the worst MLM companies, profits are usually made by signing people up, not by regularly selling actual products to real consumers. Big profits are promised for growing your "downline" or team, and climbing the "ladder" or pyramid. Illegitimate companies profit by selling start-up kits and training materials to members, not products to consumers. Making money by recruiting members is no way to run a legitimate business.

Unfortunately, unsuspecting members often pay hefty investments to join these "pyramid" style schemes. The only way that a typical MLM team member or "associate" can recover the money paid to join the business is to convince other people to join.

For an objective MLM explanation see:
https://en.wikipedia.org/wiki/Multi-level_marketing

MLMs will not help you get rich quickly, if at all. You can, however, earn good money by working hard and putting your time into building an ethical *revenue-sharing* business. Partnering with a reputable company that follows a more legit business model may generate a healthy income. It just has to be the right company, with the right products for you. Usually this takes a few years, not a few weeks as many companies claim.

Be leery of any business that promises "Quick Payouts" and "Huge Returns" or "Two Year Retirement."

If you've ever been lured into clicking by the term "Get Rich Quick," you've likely found an illegitimate business opportunity. If you encounter a company that guarantees a certain amount of money within a specific time frame, like "Quick Six Figure Income" – run! Companies promoting these unrealistic benefits are most likely scams. The recruitment and advancement methods they use are often unethical, if not completely illegal ways of making money.

If you take the leap, be ready to work full-time. Growing your list, developing your approach, (sincerely) presenting the message, and supporting and training your associates takes full-time effort. The most successful network marketers also have effective people skills – not just tacky sales tactics.

RECOMMENDED READING:

I Got Scammed So You Don't Have To! How to Find Legitimate Work at Home and Random Jobs in a Scamming Economy
https://amzn.to/3qoZdwf

Top 10 Work At Home and Home-based Business Scams
http://www.scambusters.org/work-at-home.html

How to Easily Spot Work at Home Scams
http://www.wahm.com/articles/how-to-easily-spot-work-at-home-scams.html

Pyramid Schemes, by ScamWatch
http://www.scamwatch.gov.au/content/index.phtml/tag/PyramidSchemes

Multi-Level Marketing - Why it IS a Scam, 99.9999% of the time!
http://www.consumerfraudreporting.org/MLM.php

Warning signs and red flags that could alert you to a MLM scam
http://www.fraudguides.com/tips/july5.asp

> See Appendix for a chart comparing promises of MLM scams vs. legitimate revenue sharing businesses.

Home-based Marketing Businesses

So, you've done your homework and you know what to look for. You understand the time commitment and investment which may be involved when working as a remote marketing executive for a well-established legitimate company. You're ready to find one with that perfect product you love enough to use yourself. And you're ready to take on the work as an evangelist for that product and the company. Search the internet for "Home-based Business Opportunity" and you will receive millions of results within a matter of milliseconds.

> To get an idea about how quickly the "home-based business" industry has grown, consider this. For our last revision of this book in 2016 we performed that same search and wrote: "...approximately 336,000,000 results within a matter of milliseconds."
>
> We did the same search 5 years later and received about 1,650,000,000 results (0.82 seconds)
>
> By the time you read this, there may be Billions of results to weed through!

Companies offering legitimate revenue sharing with an established business model are out there, but beware! **Investigate all opportunities before getting involved with any work-from-home network marketing business.** If a company makes it difficult to even find out what it is they offer, they are likely profiting off the business model, not any actual products.

Note: We provide the following links solely to make your research efforts easier. We have either briefly researched these companies, or have known people who worked with them. We provide no recommendations, or endorsements. All information is given without warranty.

POPULAR HOME-BASED BUSINESS OPPORTUNITIES:

5LINX Premier Opportunity
http://5linx.com/
Products and services ranging from internet and phone service to cable TV and security systems.

ACN Opportunity, LLC
http://acninc.com/opportunity
Phone service, wireless, gas and electricity, merchant services, high speed internet, television, home security and automation.

Advocare Products
https://www.advocare.com/
Energy, weight-loss, nutrition, and sports performance products

Creative Memories
http://www.ahniandzoe.com/
If you love scrapbooking, become an advisor to provide simple solutions for creating prints, books, and digital albums.

Amway
http://www.amway.com/
Nutrition, bath & body, household products and more.

Beach Body Coach
http://beachbodycoach.com/
Become a personal fitness coach.

Be Epic
https://www.bepic.com/
B-Epic's line of high-performance lifestyle products was created to naturally enhance health and wellness.

Cabi
http://www.cabionline.com
Designer clothing collection sold in a relaxed home "party" environment.

Isagenix
https://www.isagenix.com/
With a 12+ year history of helping people live healthier lives, our nutritional cleansing program stands out from the crowd.

MAKING MONEY

Juice Plus Virtual Franchise
https://www.juiceplusvirtualfranchise.com/
Juice Plus+ is whole food based nutrition in a capsule and chewable form, containing juice powder concentrates fruits, vegetables and grains.

Mary Kay
http://www.marykay.com/
Skin care, makeup, fragrance, body and sun products and gifts.

Melaleuca - the Wellness Company
https://melaleuca.info
25+ year old U.S. based billion-dollar manufacturer of premium nutritional, personal care, and household products. (NOTE: We personally enjoyed Melaleuca products and made money as remote marketing executives for 7± years.)

Paw Tree
https://www.pawtree.com/pawtree/enrollment
Position yourself as an entrepreneur in the $99± billion dollar pet industry.

Youngevity
https://youngevity.com/
Multivitamins, skin care, and nutritional products.

Pampered Chef
http://www.pamperedchef.com/
Direct seller of high quality cookware and kitchen tools, a division of Berkshire Hathaway.

Plexus Worldwide
http://www.plexusworldwide.com/
Weight loss and detoxification nutritional products.

Press-A-Print International
http://www.pressaprint.com/
Advertising, marketing and specialty printing company offering equipment, training, support and flexibility.

Princess House
http://princesshouse.com/
Professional quality kitchen products for people who love to cook…and people who don't!

SBI - Solo Build it!
http://buildit.sitesell.com/
Online business and e-commerce solutions

Scentsy Fragrance
http://scentsy.com/
Home fragrance, perfume and bath and body products.

SendOut Cards
https://www.sendoutcards.com/
Personalized cards, greeting cards and gifts.

Shaklee
http://www.shaklee.com/
Weight loss, nutrition, home, beauty and personal care products.

Thirty-One Gifts
http://www.thirtyonegifts.com/
Accessory bags, purses, totes, home office and organizing items, and stationery products.

Thrive Life
https://www.thrivelife.com/
Your favorite foods, redefined! Fruits, vegetables, meats, proteins, dairy, grains and basics – nutritious, delicious, convenient.

Tupperware
https://my.tupperware.com/
Well-established distributor of storage containers, bakeware, cook's tools and more.

The Traveling Vineyard
https://www.travelingvineyard.com/
Become an independent wine consultant and work from home.

Bodē Pro Nutrition
https://www.bodepro.com/
Liquid antioxidant, energy drinks, weight loss and nutritional supplements

JR Watkins
https://www.watkins1868.com/business-opportunities
Use superior quality natural foods, personal care, home care, and old time remedies and help others enjoy their benefits.

Young Living Essential Oils
https://www.youngliving.com/
Essential oil and aromatherapy multivitamins, antioxidant support, age based nutrition, weight management, and more.

Consider this: We originally compiled the above list in 2016 with the help of fellow nomads who worked as associates for many different companies. Most of their personal links were no longer valid. We also removed many companies from the list which no longer exist. Since we prefer the <u>entrepreneurial route</u> to financial success, we did not research additional network marketing businesses for this edition of *Income Anywhere!*

The Gig Economy

The Gig Economy exploded during COVID-19. Both employees and the self or unemployed are supplementing their income with side-gigs such as driving for Lyft, delivering for Postmates and doing odd jobs via Task Rabbit. But the pandemic has also forced many more people to piece together multiple small, side-jobs to earn enough money to survive. Often referred to as side-hustle work, the gig economy promises the independence and self-determination of self-employment. Whether or not it actually delivers is a question for your local Amazon Flex driver or freelance coder.

What is the Gig Economy? (From <u>Investopedia</u>)

- ▶ The gig economy is based on flexible, temporary, or freelance jobs, often involving connecting with clients or customers through an online platform.
- ▶ The gig economy can benefit workers, businesses, and consumers by making work more adaptable to the needs of the moment and demand for flexible lifestyles.
- ▶ At the same time, the gig economy can have downsides due to the erosion of traditional economic relationships between workers, businesses, and clients.

If you're keeping your house and hitting the road, renting it out on Airbnb, VRBO, or another platform may be a different kind of side gig for you. The same is possible for storage space, or if you have an idle vehicle sitting around. If you're in an area with an on-demand scooter or bicycle company – and have a large vehicle – you may be able to start a small business providing maintenance and relocation. And if you have a medical background, consider becoming a traveling nurse or telehealth care provider.

The ability to pick and choose jobs sounds attractive. But we don't recommend relying on gig work as your only source of income. You are still at the mercy of companies that tend to treat their contractors as disposable and not worthy of the same benefits a full-employee receives. If you still want to give it a try, there are various companies, websites, and apps to help you get started.

Types of Side Gigs

This list only scratched the surface of the Gig economy. If you can dream it up, there is likely a job available for you to do as a side-gig.

- Virtual Assistant
- Writer / Transcriber / Proofreader
- Social Media Marketer
- Photographer
- Developer / Graphic Designer
- Food Delivery, Personal Shopper
- Delivery Driver (Amazon Flex etc)
- Rideshare Driver (Uber, Lyft)
- RV Transport & Delivery
- Vehicle supplier
- Dog Walker / Pet Sitting
- Baby Sitter / Elder Care
- Housesitter
- Telehealth provider
- Retail Support (secret shopper etc)

- Mover / Handyman
- Scooter Maintenance
- Product Tester
- Tutor
- Handyman
- Researcher
- Resident Host (airbnb, etc.)
- Storage Host

Gig Economy Rewards and Challenges

Making a living from Gig work can be fulfilling and rewarding. Work at it, and you may develop a reliable source of income. Consider the following information, however, before giving up your current career path or steady job to only work side gigs.

Manage gigs like running a business. You may be your own boss, but you're also responsible for paying your own taxes. If you don't withhold at least 25% of your pay and set it aside, you may be in for a big surprise come tax time. It's best to set up a system for this, or consult with a tax professional.

Open a business bank account. Don't combine your personal and business finances. That can become rather messy come tax time. A dedicated business credit card can also help you track expenses, but be careful not to accumulate debt! Upgrade your bookkeeping with tools like FreshBooks or QuickBooks to keep business related income and expenses organized and easily accessible.

Don't put all you eggs in one basket. Gig work doesn't guarantee any fixed number of hours per week, and rarely guarantees a set pay rate. Since income can vary so greatly, it's best not to rely on one gig income source for your basic living necessities. Instead, create multiple income streams for yourself by doing different gigs.

Love what you do. Don't take on any gigs just for the money. Enjoying what you do makes the time go by quicker. Besides, working with a smile on your face improves the experience of your customers. Nobody likes a grumpy Uber driver or delivery person. And for most gig jobs, happy customers give bigger tips and better reviews.

Connect and grow. Unless you want to be a gig worker the rest of your life, use every opportunity to grow your network. You never know what kind of connections your next customer, client or passenger might have for you. Deliver as much value as possible for every gig you do.

Beware of Side Hustles that Promise "Easy Cash"

With many side gigs, you might end up earning less than minimum wage after accounting for your expenses. Some, like ride-share driving or vehicle renting may even put your own personal assets at risk. With others, you may have to pay upfront fees for unnecessary services. Be sure to read the fine print. Some companies have the contractual right to take your accumulated wages, and have a history of doing so.

Survey sites are one such gig that tends to never fulfill on big promises. Mystery Shopping may sound fun, but unless you really love shopping this may not be worth your time. You might spend hours, and gas money, for a job that pays ten bucks.

There are gig apps for renting your car, which comes with its own risks. With HyreCar you can rent your car to Uber and Lyft drivers, who put on a lot of mileage, with no guarantee of reimbursement for insurance claims. It may be better to use Turo or Giggster if considering rental of your spare vehicle.

Some survey sites charge fees for training and aptitude tests before they offer jobs. Beware of any gig work arrangements that require you to accumulate a set amount of earnings before cashing out. These sites often consider your earnings as *their* income until you hit that set amount.

See our upcoming section on "micro-gigs" for further detail and better alternatives. And if you're seriously considering gig-work as your new business model, check out the SideHusl website. SideHusl researches and rates numerous online gig economy platforms and apps. Select whether you want to work, rent, or sell something and they'll show you the possibilities. For more information and ideas, take the SideHusl quiz at https://sidehusl.com.

Best Gig Apps by Category

See resource lists for website links.

- Accommodation: Vrbo
- Caregiving: Care.com
- Delivery: Postmates
- Grocery: Instacart
- Education: Outschool
- Freelance: Upwork
- Retail Services: Field Agent
- Pet Services: Rover.com
- Transportation: Lyft
- Small Jobs: Task Rabbit

Side Gig Resources & Common Platforms

Review this list of job apps and resources to find the side gig that's right for you. Find ways to make money with your car, including driving, rental, and mobile advertising. It also includes jobs like writing, tutoring, translation, customer service, healthcare, and more.

Ride Sharing Drivers & Vehicle Suppliers

Uber and Lyft are two of the most popular side gigs for making money with your vehicle. There are a few other less popular ride-share driving apps out there. And, there are various platforms and resources available for renting out your vehicle or RV.

Uber: https://www.uber.com

Lyft: https://www.lyft.com/

Getaround: https://www.getaround.com/

Avail: https://availcarsharing.com/share-my-car

Giggster: https://giggster.com/

Turo: https://turo.com/us/en/list-your-car

HyreCar: https://www.hyrecar.com/

RVshare: https://rvshare.com/list-your-rv

RV Ezy: https://www.rvezy.com/owner

Outdoorsy: https://www.outdoorsy.com/list-your-rv

Good Sam RV Rentals: https://www.rvrentals.com/list-your-rv

Delivery Drivers

Uber Eats, Door Dash, and Grub Hub are just a few of the popular food delivery platforms. Shipt, Postmates and others hire delivery drivers for just about anything else. Amazon also hires a distributed workforce of drivers for their Prime delivery fleet.

Amazon Flex: https://flex.amazon.com/

Instacart: https://instacart.careers/

Uber Eats: https://www.uber.com/deliver/

GrubHub: https://careers.grubhub.com/

Door Dash: https://www.doordash.com/dasher/signup/

Postmates: https://www.uber.com/us/en/deliver/
(Now a division of Uber.)

Dumpling: https://dumpling.us/

Favor: https://apply.favordelivery.com/

Shipt: https://www.shipt.com/

Veho: https://shipveho.com/drive/

Citizen Shipper: https://citizenshipper.com/new-drivers

RV/Trailer Transport and Delivery

For experienced RVers and people comfortable driving a big rig or hauling a trailer, many companies offer jobs to transport RVs and trailers around the country.

Camper Connection: https://thecamperconnection.com/driver/

Classic Transport: https://www.classictransport.com/

Horizon Transport: https://horizontransport.co/

Pinnacle Transport Group: https://pinnacletransportgroup.com/

Wave: https://driveforwave.com/

"Odd Jobs" and Misc. Services

Many people aren't aware of the many specialty apps for less common side gigs. With Task Rabbit you can find small jobs from assembling furniture and installing a TV, to staffing an event or helping someone move. Find retail stocking and merchandising jobs with Field Agent. Mobile mechanics can find gigs using YourMechanic. Housecleaning crews, construction workers, plumbers, and electricians can find local work with Handy, or HomeAdvisor. And there are also apps for dog walkers, scooter/bike maintenance, mystery shoppers, and more.

Task Rabbit: https://www.taskrabbit.com/become-a-tasker
Find local jobs that fit your skills and schedule.

Home Advisor: https://pro.homeadvisor.com/
The "Angi Leads" marketplace for all home/contractor services.

Handy: https://www.handy.com/
Home cleaning and handyman services.

LaborJack: https://laborjack.com/
Find landscaping, moving, and other "muscle for hire" work.

Porch: https://porch.com/
Connecting contractors with clients looking for specific services

Jiffy On Demand: https://jiffyondemand.com/
Find small home maintenance jobs.

Your Mechanic: https://www.yourmechanic.com/automotive-technician-jobs
Find local customers in needs of automotive repair.

Bird: https://www.bird.co
Scooter maintenance

Lime: https://lime.bike/juicer
Scooter maintenance

Wag: https://wagwalking.com/dog-walker
Become a dog walker with Wag.

Rover: https://www.rover.com/become-a-sitter
Get paid to play with pets

Curated: https://www.curated.com/apply/
Connect with people. Recommend gear. Get paid.

Field Agent: https://www.fieldagent.net
Mystery Shoppers, Merchandising, and Product Testing

Best Mark: https://www.bestmark.com/
Become a mystery shopper.

Secret Shopper: https://www.secretshopper.com/

Writing, Editing, Transcription & Marketing

If you have decent writing or editing skills, there are many popular platforms for finding a good paying side gig. If you're multi-lingual or are just a fast typist, translation or transcription work may be ideal for you. And with similar skills, you may be good at social media marketing.

Contena: https://www.contena.co/jobs

Contently: https://contently.com/

Skyword: https://skyword.com/

ProBlogger: https://problogger.com/jobs

Freelance Writing: https://www.freelancewriting.com/jobs

BloggingPro: https://www.bloggingpro.com/jobs

Cambridge Proofreading: https://proofreading.org/about/careers

Allegis Transcription: https://www.allegistranscription.com

Scribie: https://scribie.com/freelance-transcription

Transcribe Me: https://workhub.transcribeme.com/

Rev: https://www.rev.com/freelancers

SocialOwl: https://socialowl.com/

Virtual Assistants

Are you an admin whiz? Many people, from executives to busy parents hire virtual assistants. Below are a few leading platforms to find remote VA jobs.

Belay: https://belaysolutions.com/work-with-us

Kayla Sloan: https://kaylasloan.com/

Priority VA: https://priorityva.com/

Virtual Assist USA: https://www.virtualassistusa.com/career-openings

Babysitting, Eldercare & In-home Services

If you enjoy working with kids or caring for the elderly, consider these platforms to find babysitting or in-home care jobs near you.

Care.com: https://www.care.com/jobs

Sittercity: https://www.sittercity.com/

Urbansitter: https://www.urbansitter.com/

Visiting Angels: https://www.visitingangels.com/employment

Right At Home: https://www.rightathome.net/jobs

BrightStar Care: https://www.brightstarcare.com/

Papa Pals: https://www.joinpapa.com/pals/signup

Travel Nursing Agencies

Traveling nurse jobs are popular, too. Many credentialed nurses are hitting the road and taking advantage of resources to find temporary nursing jobs wherever they go.

TravelNursing.org: https://www.travelnursing.org

Aya Health Care: https://www.ayahealthcare.com/

Travel Nurse Across America: https://tnaa.com/

RNNetwork: https://rnnetwork.com/

Nomad Health: https://nomadhealth.com/

The Gypsy Nurse: https://www.thegypsynurse.com/

Cross Country Nurses:
https://www.crosscountrynurses.com/

IntelyCare:
https://www.intelycare.com/for-nursing-professionals/apply/

Trusted Health:
https://www.trustedhealth.com/travel-nursing-guide

Telehealth Services

Since the impact of COVID-19, the telehealth industry has grown to include many platforms offering jobs for remote healthcare providers in human and veterinary medicine and mental health experts.

Heal.com: https://heal.com/medical-team/

Pager: https://pager.com/about-us/careers

Soothe: https://www.soothe.com/careers/

Intely Care: https://www.intelycare.com/company/careers/

Talkspace: https://www.talkspace.com/join-our-network

Better Help: https://www.betterhelp.com/counselor_application/

JustAnswer: https://era.justanswer.com/

Vetster: https://vetster.com/en-us/for-vets

Personal Tutoring

Share your knowledge with these platforms to get jobs as a traditional tutor, or online music instructor.

Outschool: https://outschool.com/

VIPKid: https://www.vipkid.com/

Education First: https://careers.ef.com/

Lessonface: https://www.lessonface.com/
Provide live online music lessons.

Rent Your House or Storage Space

If you own a house, commercial property or other real estate, short term property rental can provide a steady source of income. AirBNB and VRBO are only two of many resources for renting private property. Others exist for renting available storage space, parking spots, or locations for film/video production.

Airbnb: https://www.airbnb.com/

Vrbo: https://www.vrbo.com

FlipKey (By Trip Advisor): https://rentals.tripadvisor.com/register

Couchsurfing: https://www.couchsurfing.com/

Giggster: https://giggster.com/
Rent a venue, space or location for video production

Neighbor: https://www.neighbor.com/host-signup
Get Paid to Store Things

Peer Space: https://www.peerspace.com/host
Renting your space for meetings, events, and film/photo shoots.

Share My Space: https://www.sharemyspace.com/
List your space or venue for rent.

Store At My House: https://www.storeatmyhouse.com/
Make money renting peer-to-peer Storage Space

Stashii: https://stashii.com/
Canadian peer-to-peer storage and parking marketplace.

Get Paid to Advertise on Your RV or Car

If you don't mind putting decals, window stickers, or a wrap on your vehicle, car advertising companies will pay you to advertise on your car. These firms partner with companies to produce fleet graphics that get applied to private cars.

Some car advertisers will ship you a small decal to apply. Others will require you to have your car wrapped by professional installers. The company then verifies installation of the decal and pays you for set periods of time. The amount of money you can earn with car advertising varies greatly. Potential income may depend upon the length of the campaign, size of the decal/wrap, and whether or not you receive a commission.

Like many home-based business opportunities, scams

are rampant in the car wrap industry. Closely research any company to make sure it's legitimate before you agree to sign up. Signs of reputable companies include:

- A formal application process.
- Evaluation of your car model and condition.
- Driving history review and background check.
- Require owners to provide proof of auto insurance.
- And will not charge an application fee.

MOBILE ADVERTISING RESOURCES:

Nickelytics
https://www.nickelytics.com/drive/

Stickr
http://www.stickr.co/

Sticker Ride
https://stickerride.com/ads/drivers

Wrapify
https://wrapify.com/drive/

Carvertise
https://carvertise.com/drivers/

Get Paid to Advertise on Your Car
https://worldscholarshipforum.com/wealth/get-paid-to-advertise-on-your-car/

RECOMMENDED READING

Side Hustle: From Idea to Income in 27 Days
https://amzn.to/3dpbkC3

The Side Hustle: Turn Your Spare Time into $1000 a Month
https://amzn.to/3xXr3BK

So You Want to Start a Side Hustle
https://amzn.to/3y2nudF

SideHusl
https://sidehusl.com/
Reviews and rates more than 350 online side-hustle job platforms.

25 Best Gig Economy Jobs for Earning Supplemental Income
https://dollarsprout.com/gig-economy-jobs/

Join the Talent Marketplace

If you have experience as a developer, graphic designer, SEO Expert, or other professional, there are dozens of online marketplaces to find freelance work. The competition is stiff on these sites. If you're used to charging top dollar for your services, you may need to reevaluate your rates. But the benefits include access to many potential side jobs.

Thousands of people every day search for someone to help with their website or a logo for their new small business. The types of clients who search sites like Fiverr are often looking for a bargain. But they need you. And many are also looking to partner with someone who can help them for the long run. Do good on one gig, and it may likely lead to another.

With platforms that provide easy payment, marketing, customer reviews and more, talent marketplaces can open up numerous opportunities.

Fiverr

The original concept of Fiverr was connecting people with freelancers providing specific services for as little as five dollars. That may not sound like much, but it gets clients knocking on your door. For example, consider our experience working with Fiverr talent. A transcriptionist we regularly use provides a high quality transcription service with quick turnaround for our Tripawd Talk Radio podcast episodes. She charges $5 for 10 minutes of audio. Right on her Fiverr page, we can enter the number of minutes and see what it will cost to transcribe an entire episode. ($30 for 60 minutes and two speakers.) Try building that functionality on your own website, and marketing your services, and reaching an audience as big as Fiverr's! Join the thousands of freelancers on the site and you can craft your service bundles on their platform, which makes it easy for clients to find and work with you.

Upwork

This is a talent marketplace that we believe provides a higher caliber of service than Fiverr. From design, development, and IT to legal assistance, sales, and marketing, Upwork enables freelancers to craft comprehensive projects for hire. The platform also lets clients write up their project details, allowing the marketplace to bid on jobs. Again, with all the marketing, project management, invoicing, and payment built into the platform, it's another talent marketplace making it easy for you to list your services.

Other Talent Marketplaces

Certain marketplaces, like Crowdspring and 99 Designs provide access to crowdsourced talent. Clients may hire someone for a specific job, or start a contest. They'll then post their creative brief or project specs and budget. Service providers then present their work, only getting paid if their design is selected. Be sure to consider what your services and your time are worth when throwing your hat in the ring with these talent marketplaces.

Below you will find many job marketplaces specifically for digitally minded creative types such as graphic artists, designers, and photographers. In addition, many enable artists to market and sell their work to the public. You'll also find online marketplaces where you can sell your photography, website/design templates, blog themes, and other audio/visual assets.

TALENT & DESIGN MARKETPLACES

Fiverr
https://www.fiverr.com/start_selling
Work Your Way

Upwork
https://www.upwork.com/
Join the world's work marketplace

99Designs
https://99designs.com/designers
Fire up your freelance career

DesignCrowd
https://www.designcrowd.com/
Find design clients and build your freelance career.

Crowdsprping
https://www.crowdspring.com/register/
Join as a designer or namer.

Design Contest
https://www.designcontest.com/
Pitch your creativity to contest holders.

Logo My Way
https://www.logomyway.com/designerRegister.php
Sell logos and compete in design contests.

Logo Tournament
https://logotournament.com/
Compete in design contests to get paid.

Hatchwise
https://www.hatchwise.com/
Crowdsourced design and naming contests.

Zillion Designs
https://www.zilliondesigns.com/
Business Logo Design Contest Marketplace

CREATIVE & DEVELOPMENT JOB PORTALS

Freelancer
https://www.freelancer.com/
Find jobs to fit your skills.

Guru
https://www.guru.com/
Worldwide clients searching for freelance talent.

Krop
https://www.krop.com/
Showcase your work and find creative jobs/

HubStaff Talent
https://talent.hubstaff.com/work
Access to clients looking for freelancers.

Envato Studio
https://studio.envato.com/
Connect with clients needing design or development.

Stack Overflow Jobs:
https://stackoverflow.com/jobs
For Developers First

Creative Heads
https://www.creativeheads.net/
Video, gaming and animation job board

Programmer Meet Designer
http://programmermeetdesigner.com/
Connects Web Developers with Designers & Writers

SELL YOUR CREATIVE ASSETS AND WARES

Inkd: https://inkd.com/sell/
Sell customizable design files in popular software formats.

BrandCrowd: https://www.brandcrowd.com/
Turn your logos and icon designs into money.

Fantero: https://www.fantero.com/
Sell your photos and design assets.

Envato: https://author.envato.com
Popular community for selling your creative and development work.

Theme Forest by Envato: https://themeforest.net/
Sell WordPress Themes & Website Templates

SELL YOUR PHOTOGRAPHY

iStock: https://www.istockphoto.com/
Sell your photos, graphics and video.

Adobe Stock: https://contributor.stock.adobe.com/
Sell your content to the world's largest creative community.

Shutterstock; https://submit.shutterstock.com/
Share your work and start earning.

Alamy: https://www.alamy.com/contributor/
Get your images seen by image buyers around the world.

Smug Mug: https://www.smugmug.com/
Secure platform for selling photo prints and downloads.

PicFair: https://www.picfair.com/
The beautifully simple way to sell your images.

Photo Shelter; https://www.photoshelter.com/
Create your photo website, and sell or license your photos

Tour Photos: https://tourphotos.com/
Platform dedicated to selling tourism photos.

ZenFolio: https://zenfolio.com/
All-in-one website to show, share & sell your photography.

Snapped4u: https://snapped4u.com
The easy way to sell event photography and portraits!

Foap: https://www.foap.com/photographer
Fulfill photo missions or upload photos and videos for sale.

500px: https://500px.com/
Create your own photography website in minutes.

FotoMoto: https://www.fotomoto.com/
Print-on-demand e-commerce widget for your website.

SELL DESIGNS ON APPAREL AND GIFTS
Zazzle: https://www.zazzle.com/

Spreadshirt: https://www.spreadshirt.com/

Threadless: https://www.threadless.com/

Cafe Press: https://www.cafepress.com/

Teepublic: https://www.teepublic.com/

Teespring: https://teespring.com/

Printfection: https://www.printfection.com/

Kotis Design: https://kotisdesign.com

Yizzam: https://yizzam.com/

Gelato: https://gelato.com/
Sell direct or connect to Etsy, Shopify, WooCommerce and more.

Other Freelance Work Resources for Side-Hustle Jobs

Remote work job portals can help you find freelance projects. These portals range from "contest" style graphic design marketplaces like CrowdSpring to job bidding sites that award projects to the lowest bidders.

Many employment sites, however, have sections dedicated to full-time and contract freelance work. Others like Upwork and oDesk are specifically designed for the remote workforce. Many sites are free to join while even some legitimate ones charge registration fees, or commissions based on the amount of an awarded project. Intro-U is one platform that provides job search and community features without charging fees.

FREELANCE & REMOTE JOB PORTALS

Freelancer: https://www.freelancer.com/

Fiverr: https://www.fiverr.com/start_selling

Upwork: https://www.upwork.com/

oDesk: https://odeskwork.com/

Toptal: https://www.toptal.com/

Intro-U: https://www.introu.co/

Monster: https://www.monster.com/

SimplyHired: https://www.simplyhired.com/

Authentic Jobs: https://authenticjobs.com/

People Per Hour: https://www.peopleperhour.com/

Freelancer Map: https://www.freelancermap.com/

Sykes: https://jobs.sykes.com/

Idealist: https://www.idealist.org

Working Not Working: https://workingnotworking.com

The Muse: https://www.themuse.com/

We Work Remotely: https://weworkremotely.com/

Skip The Drive: https://www.skipthedrive.com/

Bunny Studio: https://bunnystudio.com/

Power to Fly: https://powertofly.com/

Virtual Vocations: https://www.virtualvocations.com/

Working Nomads: https://www.workingnomads.co/jobs

Freelance Auction: https://www.freelanceauction.com/

Remote Programming Jobs: https://remotive.io/

Ruby / Rails Jobs: https://jobs.rubynow.com/

Stack Overflow: https://stackoverflow.com/jobs

Work At Home Desk: http://workathomedesk.com/

Rat Race Rebellion: https://ratracerebellion.com/

FOR THE WORK AT HOME MOM
Work At Home Mom Revolution
https://workathomemomrevolution.com/

The Work At Home Woman
https://www.theworkathomewoman.com

The Mom Project
https://themomproject.com/

Work At Home Mom Magazine
https://www.wahm.com/

The Flexwork for Women Alliance
https://www.kathrynsollmann.com/the-flexwork-women-alliance/

Finding Work to Fit Your Unique Talent

Specialty job search engines and platforms to earn from your expertise also exist. Become a tutor with Outschool or teach English to kids on VIP Kid. Join one of the many education marketplaces like Teachable or Udemy to create your own courses or become a coach. Or, use a platform like Kajabi to build your coaching business or membership site with everything you need.

TEACHING PORTALS AND ONLINE CLASS RESOURCES
Platforms to teach online or start a coaching business.

Amava: Setup your classroom on Amava.
https://amava.com/become/guide

Udemy: Teach online, share your knowledge.
https://www.udemy.com/teaching/

Teachable: Create online courses and coaching services.
https://teachable.com/

Thinkific: Create and sell online courses and memberships.
https://www.thinkific.com/

Skillshare: https://www.skillshare.com/teach
Teach on Skillshare and share your passion.

Fizzle: Earn a living doing something you love.
https://fizzle.co/

Kajabi: Create and sell online courses and coaching.
https://kajabi.com/

Outschool: Inspire a love of learning and earn.
https://outschool.com/

Coursera: Teach for 200+ leading universities and companies.
https://www.coursera.org/

Lessonface: Teach live online music lessons.
https://www.lessonface.com/

VIP Kid: Teach English online from the comfort of home.
https://www.vipkidteachers.com/teach

Preply: Become an online language tutor.
https://preply.com/

Ed2Go: Develop online courses about any subject.
https://www.ed2go.com/TeachWithUs.aspx

Edureka: Become an instructor with online training company.
https://www.edureka.co/instructors/add

Mirasee: Launch a course or learn from the experts.
https://mirasee.com/

Freelancing Outside the Box

Got a specific talent or want to think outside the usual job search box? You'll find many portals and resources to find specific job types with a quick search for your talent keywords. Online cooking lessons or singing coach? There's probably a marketplace out their for your services. Consider the following specialty job sites for everything from call center jobs and retail stocking or plumbing and electrical service, to social media marketing and voice-over acting.

SPECIALTY FREELANCE JOB SITES

Pro Referral: https://www.proreferral.com/
The home improvement project job portal.

WAHVE: https://wahve.com/
Work At Home Vintage Experts: Jobs for Pretiring Professionals

Solo Gig: https://www.sologig.com/
Find Engineering and IT Jobs

The Voice Realm: http://freelancevoiceactors.com/
Freelance voice-over acting jobs.

Voicebunny.com: https://bunnystudio.com/voice/
Jobs for voice-over actors.

MarketHire: https://marketerhire.com/
The best way to level up your freelance marketing career

Social Owl: https://socialowl.com/
Start a social media marketing business.

Live Ops: https://www.liveops.com/
Virtual/remote call center jobs.

Sitel: https://www.sitel.com/careers/work-from-home-jobs/
Work from Home Customer Service Jobs

Working Solutions: https://workingsolutions.com/
Outsourced Customer Service Solutions

Jyve: https://jyve.com/
Retail stocking, auditing, and merchandising

WTG Merchandising: https://www.wtgmerch.com/
Flexible retail merchandising jobs.

Ejury: https://www.ejury.com/
Participate in mock trials and focus groups.

Online Verdict: https://www.onlineverdict.com/jurors/
Get paid to review and respond to legal cases.

Human Domain Solutions: https://work4hds.com/
Casualty role playing jobs for disaster management training.

BioLife: https://www.biolifeplasma.com/
Donate plasma and earn up to $800 per month.

Micro Jobs and the Truth About Taking Surveys

A small segment of internet based gig jobs include consists of "micro-jobs," which entail completing small tasks for small pay. All of these jobs will require a computer and internet access. Examples include:

▶ Taking short surveys

▶ Cleaning up text documents and spreadsheets.

▶ Collect data, edit product listings, or correct AI-generated speech to text translations.

- Refine Machine Learning and Artificial Intelligence applications, without technical development skills.
- Transcribe audio and video files, usually in 10 minutes or less – starting as low as $5 per hour pay rate.
- Personal virtual assistant jobs that can pay from $3 to $7 per task like booking a dinner reservation or calling the cable company.
- If you are multilingual, you may be able to provide manual translation services.
- Gamers may be able to get paid testing the latest immersive gaming experience.

Micro tasks come with micro pay.

Microtasking is one of the easiest forms of gig economy jobs. But it also pays the least amount. This not exactly an income method to rely upon for supporting your lifestyle and building wealth. It is more appropriate to fill any small pockets of time throughout your day, when you may earn a few bucks – often cents – for fulfilling some rather mindless duties.

Before you dive in, ask yourself: What is your time worth? Consider signing up for these jobs if you often have a long bus ride, or spend afternoons waiting to pick up the kids from school. Reserve these micro-paying tasks for when your other money-earning options are limited, or if you have free time on your hands.

POPULAR MICRO-JOB SITES
Amazon Mechanical Turk: https://www.mturk.com/
Make money in spare time. Get paid for completing simple tasks.

Clickworker: https://www.clickworker.com/clickworker/
Profit from your talents.

Appen: https://appen.com/
Part-time flexible work that can be done from anywhere.

Atexto: https://landing.atexto.com/jobs
Audio transcription and voice recording.

Scribie: https://scribie.com/freelance-transcription
Audio/Video Transcription Service

Lionbridge: https://www.lionbridge.com/join-our-team/
Your voice counts. Your insights are welcome.

Fancy Hands: https://www.fancyhands.com/
Fancy Hands offers virtual assistants to everyone.

Inbox Dollars: https://www.inboxdollars.com/
Earn Cash for Your Everyday Online Activities

Voicepark: https://www.voicepark.com/
Contribute to the development of products and services in the consumer marketplace.

Swagbucks: https://www.swagbucks.com/
Get Free Gift Cards & Cash for the everyday things you do online.

Cash Crate: https://www.cashcrate.com
Find Vetted Opportunities To Make Money Online

TVision Panel: https://www.mytvpanel.com/applyform
Earn money and help the TV industry understand what makes you tune in.

SVOD Voice: https://www.svodvoice.com/
get rewarded to help shape the Streaming Video on Demand industry.

Google Opinion Rewards:
https://play.google.com/store/apps/details?id=com.google.android.apps.paidtasks
Answer quick surveys and earn Google Play credit with an Android app.

Getting Paid for Product Reviews and Surveys

You may have heard that you can make money taking surveys. Well sure you can, sort of. What is your time worth? Some of the most popular micro-jobs are offered by market research companies that promise rewards for taking short surveys. Again, this is **not** something you'll want to focus on as a primary source of income. And for many of these opportunities, that income may be in the form of gift cards instead of cash. If you have time to fill, you may be able to make a few cents for a few minutes of your time.

This "work" requires no skill whatsoever. It also pays very little. But if you view it as a fun way to supplement your primary income methods it can be rewarding. Jim decided to determine the truth about taking surveys, and this is what he found out.

The majority of survey sites operate on a points based system. Most don't explain this clearly before you sign up. With the popular survey site CrowdTap for instance, completing the average survey may earn you from three to thirty points. Answering these simple questions may take you from two to ten minutes. Most questions are multiple choice, but longer surveys ask for written feedback. Simple enough, right? But do the math. When it comes time to redeem your points, the minimum reward is a $5 Gift Card. You cannot redeem points for cash, but you can get an Amazon gift card or save at Target, Starbucks, Walmart, Olive Garden, or many other retail partners. And that $5 gift card? It will cost you 1,000 points.

Over the course of about eight weeks, Jim earned enough points (5,000) to get us $25 in Amazon store credit. Great, that's some fun money we didn't have. But overall, it probably took him a total of six hours, completing surveys a few minutes at a time. That's about $4.17 per hour. As a marketer and graphic designer, he did enjoy providing feedback on new packaging design concepts. These usually took a bit longer, and rewarded up to 90 points. Oh boy! He now only periodically uses CrowdTap during the rare free time he occasionally enjoys. It's simply a relatively productive way to fill time while waiting in line or traveling as a passenger. Eventually we may have enough points for a monthly supply of RV toilet paper from Walmart.

POPULAR SURVEY SITES

CrowdTap: https://crowdtap.com/
Earn cool rewards for giving honest feedback.

Survey Junkie: https://www.surveyjunkie.com/
Take surveys. Get paid.

Branded Surveys: https://surveys.gobranded.com/paid-surveys/
Take Online Paid Surveys and Start Earning Money With Branded.

Rakuten: https://member.insight.rakuten.us/
Get paid taking online surveys anytime, anywhere.

YouGov Global: https://account.yougov.com/us-en/join/main
Share your opinion on politics, sports, entertainment and more.

Capterra: https://review.capterra.com/search-social-a/
Earn rewards by sharing your experience with software.

Reward Bee: https://www.rewardbee.com/
Reward yourself with fan-favorite prizes by completing surveys, playing games

American Consumer Opinion; https://www.acop.com/
Get paid to answer online surveys.

Flash Rewards: https://flashrewards.co/
Get rewarded in a flash.

Univox: https://www.univoxcommunity.com/
Take surveys, Earn Rewards!

Opinaia: https://opinaia.com/
Share your opinion and get rewards.

Premium Surveys: https://mypremiumsurvey.com
Earn rewards with online surveys

Life Points: https://www.lifepointspanel.com/
Free Paid Surveys & Rewards

I Say: https://i-say.com
Share your opinion with i-Say and earn rewards.

BizRate Rewards: https://www.bizraterewards.com/
Take surveys to earn rewards.

Drumo: https://drumo.com/
Get paid for your opinion

NiceQuest: https://www.nicequest.com/
Share the moment. Get rewarded

Opinions for Good:
https://go.opinions4good.com/businessprofessionals
Get Paid To Share Your Insights

PRODUCT REVIEW SITES:

User Testing
https://www.usertesting.com/get-paid-to-test
Get paid to share your perspective with global brands

Nice Discount
https://www.nicediscount.net/
Amazon.com Product Tester Club

Forthright
https://www.beforthright.com/
At Forthright, you take surveys, you get rewarded.

Capterra
https://review.capterra.com/search-social-a
Write Software Review for Rewards

Communa
https://www.communa.com/
Give Your Opinion. Earn Rewards

G2
https://www.g2.com/
Write software reviews for rewards.

IstaPanel
https://instapanel.com/
Market research for leading brands.

GetApp
https://review.getapp.com/search-social
Review Business Software.

My Points
https://www.mypoints.com/
Earn Points by shopping at your favorite stores

How Survey Sites Can Pay Off

Doing his survey site research, Jim discovered resources that can pay well for a minimal amount of time. Market Research companies ask for a bit more of your time, and require knowledge on a specific subject. They host interviews for clients to gain user feedback or input on new products in development. We have both participated in

Dscout "missions" that have earned us a few hundred dollars. These tasks required us to use a new feature on a website or app, either on our own or in real-time during a video conference. We would then summarize our feedback on the call, or by completing questionnaires and submitting a video describing our experience.

Most Dscout missions require using their mobile app. And, "scouts" must apply for missions which usually requires asking questions and submitting a selfie video about your experience on the subject. Mission topics range from health care and insurance, to gardening, technology, and travel. Jim even earned $75 for a four-part mission about Recreational Vehicles, which took him less than an hour to complete.

Jim has also participated in live one on one market research video interviews with Askable and The Expert Cafe. These sessions normally last about an our, and have paid as much as $150. Grape Data is another market research firm that will pay for interviews, even if you're not an expert on the subject. They make it easy for you to interview professionals in specific positions by phone. Then you get paid by submitting the results and proof of your call.

POPULAR MARKET RESEARCH SITES

DScout: https://dscout.com/be-a-scout
Get rewarded for sharing your experience

Expert Cafe: https://theexpertcafe.com/
Share your opinion. Get Rewarded. Shape the Future.

Grape Data: https://www.grape-data.com/contributors
Expert or Consumer Questionnaires & Online Interviews.

Askable: https://www.askable.com
Paid research opportunities, when it suits you.

Slice Market Research: https://slicemr.com/slice-rewards.php
influence future products and services by sharing your opinions

Angus Reid: https://www.angusreidusa.com/
Share your views and opinions on a variety of topics.

Zintro: https://www.zintro.com
Become an expert for market research and project work.

Money 4 Talk: https://money4talk.com/
Get paid to talk.

Qmee: https://www.qmee.com/
Share your Opinion & Shop to earn real cash rewards.

Product Lab: https://productlab.ai/
Share insights, get paid.

Cocoon: https://getcocoon.com/data_rewards
Earn cash for everyday browsing.

2020 Research: https://join.2020panel.com/
Get paid for sharing your opinion.

RECOMMENDED READING

69 Legit Ways To Get Paid
https://www.carefulcents.com/i-need-money/

50 Best Job Sites for Freelancers and Independent Professionals
https://www.hongkiat.com/blog/50-freelance-job-sites-for-designers-programmers-best-of/

How To Find Legitimate Work-From-Home Jobs
https://clark.com/employment-military/work-home-guide/

Your Gift Card Balance: $152.53

Reload Your Balance   Redeem a Gift Card

Your Auto-Reload Setting
Auto-Reload on a schedule or when your balance gets low.
Set up Auto-Reload

Gift Card Activity Page 1 of 5 (75 total transactions)

Date	Description	Amount
January 7, 2022	Payment towards Amazon.com order	-$16.15
January 5, 2022	Payment towards Amazon.com order	-$87.26
December 19, 2021	Gift card claim (claim code xxxx-xxxxxx-EFAP)	$5.00
December 13, 2021	Gift card claim (claim code xxxx-xxxxxx-JWAY)	$15.00
December 6, 2021	Gift card claim (claim code xxxx-xxxxxx-D8A5)	$100.00
November 30, 2021	Gift card claim (claim code xxxx-xxxxxx-G9AU)	$10.00
November 28, 2021	Gift card claim (claim code xxxx-xxxxxx-ZNA8)	$20.00
November 28, 2021	Gift card claim (claim code xxxx-xxxxxx-LGAS)	$5.00

Taking surveys can pay off with some extra fun money over time, but should not be considered a reliable source of income.

> When we first married, my wife and I were DINKs (double income, no kids). Then we found ourselves in a commuter marriage. When that didn't work, we became a DINJ couple (double income, no jobs). We're not alone. Dennis Benson, whom I introduced in Chapter 4, runs his Appropriate Solutions microbusiness with his wife, Sandy. Rene Agredano and her husband, Jim Nelson, left jobs in Silicon Valley to become partners in a home-based marketing business in rural Eureka, California. "I got tired being in my car for two to three hours a day, going to a job where I was busting my butt for a living," Agredano told me. And Carole and Geoffrey Howard are veritable veterans. Geoffrey has been a free agent training consultant for twenty-four years, Carole for eighteen. They work together on training projects, sitting side by side in a home office that overlooks woodlands in Warwick, New York. They also maintain a few separate clients so they don't suffocate each other. "We've collaborated on our free agency for twenty years and on our marriage for thirty," Geoffrey told me, "and so far, so good. But we think that means we're entitled to celebrate our fiftieth anniversary this year."
>
> Again, free agent couplehood is nothing new. Before the industrial economy, spouses often worked together. Just as those small shopkeepers lived above the store, my family—with Dad's third-floor office—lives below the store. And thanks to the Internet, Mom and Pop's operation doesn't have to be a mom-andpop operation. Just ask Julia and Michael Thomas of Washington, D.C. They operate a small Internet venture called Zoomsearch

Rene shared insight in an interview with author Daniel Pink for his 2001 book, Free Agent Nation – shortly after we first started our self employment journey.

> *If you understand the independent worker, the self-employed professional, the freelancer, the e-lancer, the temp, you understand how work and business in the U.S. operate today."*
> – DANIEL PINK, AUTHOR OF FREE AGENT NATION: HOW AMERICA'S NEW INDEPENDENT WORKERS ARE TRANSFORMING THE WAY WE LIVE
> HTTPS://AMZN.TO/35YJGAD

> *If achieving success were easy, more people would do it."*
> – GUY KAWASAKI, AUTHOR OF APE: AUTHOR, PUBLISHER, ENTREPRENEUR. HOW TO PUBLISH A BOOK
> HTTPS://AMZN.TO/3B9FVOX

> *Instead of wondering when your next vacation is, maybe you should set up a life you don't need to escape from.*
> – SETH GODIN, AUTHOR OF PURPLE COW, NEW EDITION: TRANSFORM YOUR BUSINESS BY BEING REMARKABLE
> HTTPS://AMZN.TO/3358WII

SELF-EMPLOYMENT

Should You Start Your Own Business?

If you dream about starting a business you can work from anywhere, you're not alone. Since the pandemic began, the numbers of people taking the leap to self-employed life continue skyrocketing. According to the U.S. Bureau of Labor Statistics, 10.9% of workers (9.65 million) were self-employed in 2020, the highest amount seen in the last three years. And not all are tech-savvy nerds either. The most popular self-employment jobs and careers include self-enrichment teachers and coaches, barbers and hair stylists, massage therapists, animal caretakers, mechanics, plumbers and electricians, and sales reps.

The options to make money on the road are only limited by your imagination and your drive to succeed. If you can see yourself as an entrepreneur, what type of business would make you happiest? Consider the following questions about starting a small business:

- ▶ Do you already have the skills to start this business?
- ▶ Do you have connections in the industry?
- ▶ Can you afford to take a pay cut while you grow the business?
- ▶ Can it be done on the road in the RV you want to buy?
- ▶ How much money do you need to get it launched?
- ▶ Will it pay your bills and support your lifestyle?

Why We Believe Self-employment Is the Way to Go

Do you know what letters in the word "JOB" stand for? Just. Over. Broke.

Studies show that on average, the net worth of a self-employed individual is considerably higher than someone who relies on a paycheck from an employer. While many jobs offer advancement in the ranks with corresponding pay hikes, eventually every employee hits a wage ceiling. Self-employed people, on the other hand, have no limits to how much they can earn. Ditching a paycheck for the uncertainty of self-employment is risky, but unless you try it you'll never know if it can put you on your path to financial and personal freedom.

The Rewards of Being Self-Employed

- You are your own boss (but you serve your customers and clients)
- You'll never get another lay-off notice
- Yes, you really can make your own work schedule
- You are free to do work that brings you (and others) joy and fulfillment
- It's so nice to work without someone looking over your shoulder
- A great accountant can uncover legit small business breaks to lower your taxable income
- Nearly everything in your life from travel to cars to your home is a potential write-off!

The Downside of Being Self-Employed

- You are your own boss (you must hold yourself accountable)
- You're always searching for new clients and customers
- Managing existing clients to keep revenue flowing is never-ending
- No more separation between work and personal life
- Some years are a constant struggle between feast-and-famine
- You will work harder and longer than ever before to keep money coming in.

liveworkdream.com

We left the corporate world to work for ourselves 25 years ago, and we'll never go back. We've discovered that the benefits of growing your own business are as limitless as the number of home-based business opportunities available. But before you make the leap, do your homework. Only you can fully assess the possibilities for your own success and know what you're getting into, financially and mentally. Most importantly, be passionate about whatever it is you decide to do. Better yet, find your purpose and fulfill it every day. Do what you love and you will do it well. In turn, you'll make good money.

Our opinion is that the most effective and fulfilling way toward personal and financial freedom is to take charge of your future and operate your own microenterprise. But not everyone has what it takes to do that. Do you?

If you do what you love, you'll never work a day in your life.
– MARC ANTHONY

Small Business You Can Do Anywhere

You have some sort of talent. Everyone is an expert at something. You know more about at least one subject than others do. That makes you an expert compared to them. And you can turn your expertise into a business. With the right skillset and tools, you can become self-employed and do these jobs just about anywhere. You might provide in-person services locally, or online via your own website.

With proper planning and enough ambition to succeed, you can build a road-worthy career as a self-employed person. Examples include:

▶ Accounting and Tax Preparation
▶ Advertising Sales
▶ Antiques/Collectibles Dealer

SELF-EMPLOYMENT

- Auto Detailing and RV Cleaning
- Business or Life Coach
- E-Course Instructor
- Computer Programmer
- Computer Training and Technical Support
- Crime Scene Cleanup Technician
- Customer Service Phone Representative
- Direct Product Sales
- DJ or Musician
- Dog Groomer
- Dog Trainer
- Electrician
- English Teacher
- Event Planning and Promotion
- Financial Planning
- Fitness Trainer
- Gift Basket Designer
- Graphic Designer
- Hair Stylist
- Home Cleaning
- Home Healthcare Aide
- Hypnotherapist
- Illustrator
- Independent Sales Representative
- Interpreter or Translator
- Jewelry Designer
- Marketing Consultant
- Mobile Auto/RV Repair
- Massage Therapist
- Personal Chef or Caterer
- Personal Trainer
- Pet Sitting and Dog Walking
- Photography and Video Production
- Plumber/Handyman
- Product Marketing or Sales
- Professional Organizer
- Proofreader
- Publication Ad Sales
- Research
- Resume Preparation
- RV Technician
- Seamstress
- Social Media or SEO Expert
- Solar Power Technician
- Technical Writer
- Traveling Nurse
- Tutoring
- Virtual Assistant
- Web Development
- Writing and Editing
- And More!

This list is by no means complete. **Your potential as an entrepreneur is only limited by your imagination and drive to succeed.**

Step 1: Find Your Purpose Then Follow Your Passion

Many successful entrepreneurs and coaches have recommended building your business around your passion. Everyone is passionate about something. You may be passionate about model trains, muscle cars, or making gift baskets. All of these could be built into a home-based business. But to be truly fulfilling – and therefore, financially successful – that passion must also serve others. We're talking about finding purpose, our own personal reason for being. The Japanese refer to this as Ikigai (sounds like "Icky Guy").

Ikigai is the concept often used to identify the source of value in one's life, or the things that make one's life worthwhile. It also entails serving others. For example, we have a friend and colleague who started her own home-based business making gift baskets. That was her passion. The enterprise really took off once she shifted gears to helping other people grow their own gift basket businesses. That is her purpose. Shirley George Frazier is now the leading authority in how to start a gift basket business. By doing what she loves, and helping others, she has found success and fulfillment while working from home.

What is your purpose? It all starts with asking: Why? Once you nail down why you do what you do, you are on the right track to building a fulfilling, successful business. But it can't be all about the money. Starting a certain business only because you think it will make you rich will likely result in stress and failure. Ask yourself how what you offer will help others. By defining your purpose, with a little passion and proper planning, you will be on the road to success.

Dr. Rangan Chatterjee has some very helpful tips and specific steps one can take toward living a more fulfilled, stress-free life – one with meaning and purpose. He sums it up with the acronym, L.I.V.E.: Love. Intention. Vision. Engagement.

> *Find something you love doing, so it becomes your reason for getting up in the morning."*
> – DR. RANGAN CHATTERJEE

We love what we do. It is the reason we get up every morning. Our Ikigai is rather specific, much like the micro-niche business we have built for ourselves. Maintaining Tripawds – the largest online support community for three-legged pets and their people – helps pay the bills, but it doesn't exactly feel like a J-O-B. It is simply what we're meant to do. We may not particularly enjoy the grind of certain tasks we must perform on a daily basis, but knowing it is done in the service of others makes it all worthwhile.

RECOMMENDED READING

Writing Prompt Journal: How To Find Your Purpose In Life?
https://amzn.to/3F5UUu0

You Deserve To Love Your Job: How to find your purpose & enjoy your life
https://amzn.to/3DbQnFl

Find Your Passion: 7 simple steps to find your purpose and carry out the job you want
https://amzn.to/3F8y4St

How to L.I.V.E More
https://drchatterjee.com/l-v-e/

L.I.V.E. a More Fulfilled Life with Your Icky Guy
https://liveworkdream.com/2020/01/01/ikigai/

> *Do what you love; you'll be better at it.*
> – LL COOL J

> *Do what you love and the money will follow.*
> – MARSHA SINETAR

Common Attributes of Successful Self-Employed People

Purpose and passion alone do not guarantee success. The term "it takes a village" holds true for growing a profitable business as much it does for nurturing a child to grow in a safe and healthy environment. When going the self-employment route, however, we don't always have the whole village on our side. As a married couple driven by the same purpose, we're fortunate to have two of us working together toward the same goals. We divide our tasks according to our talents and work together as a team. But the typical solopreneur often must go it alone.

As chief, cook, and bottle washer, the newly self-employed person takes on all roles from janitor to CEO. Otherwise, they must have the resources to build a team for product development, marketing, management, accounting, and everything else to get the business going. With this in mind, there are certain characteristics common among successful entrepreneurs including:

Technical Aptitude

In addition to the technical capabilities required to create and deliver your product, you also need a certain level of technological savvy – or at least the willingness and ability to quickly learn new software and online platforms.

Communications Skills

You alone may be responsible for developing your business plan, creating your product or service, launching your website, marketing it to the world, and managing the books. This requires a firm grasp on written language, project management, and good communication skills for starters.

Time Management Skills

As a self-employed person, the ability to focus without distraction is imperative. Planning and successfully accomplishing your business goals requires good time management skills. You also must be able to troubleshoot any issues that may arise.

Determination, Drive, and Spirit

You can make up much of what you lack in any department with a strong desire to get the job done and knowing where to look for help. This takes good critical thinking skills. That's the ability to look at the big picture, as it really is. Dissect it into parts and tasks that you can accomplish, or delegate to others.

A Willingness to Learn from Mistakes

You will face challenges as you grow your business – many of them. You'll need to figure them out, and know when to ask for help. Successful entrepreneurs must understand how to evaluate their accomplishments and learn from their mistakes. Only by reviewing our progress and adjusting our goals can we continue to grow a business that sustains our lifestyle and allows us to build savings for the future.

Profitable self-employed people perform consistently, with perseverance. As James Clear explains in his acclaimed book, <u>Atomic Habits</u>, being successful means focusing on systems, not goals. That's because both winners and losers have the same goals. For instance, all runners want to win the race. For those who fail to succeed, the problem isn't with the goals they set, it lies in the systems they put in place and whether or not they followed through with the plan.

Think you have what it takes to fulfill your purpose and turn it into a profitable business? Read on for some helpful tips we've learned along the road to self-employment success.

> *Ever tried. Ever failed. No matter. Try again. Fail again.* ***Fail better.***
> – SAMUEL BECKET
> HTTPS://AMZN.TO/3UWV00E

The Solopreneur's Toolkit:

- Purpose (Ikigai)
- Technical Capabilities
- Time Management Skills
- Determination, Drive & Spirit
- Critical Thinking & Troubleshooting
- Perseverance, Consistency & Follow-through

RECOMMENDED READING:

Start: Punch Fear in the Face, Escape Average, and Do Work That Matters
https://amzn.to/3qrEcRP

Atomic Habits – An Easy and Proven Way to Build Good Habits and Break Bad ones
https://amzn.to/3kuBLKA

Starting a Business QuickStart Guide: The Simplified Beginner's Guide to Launching a Successful Small Business
https://amzn.to/3kqntKM

The Entrepreneur's Survival Handbook: A Deck of 52 Insightful Pointers from an Experienced Entrepreneur
https://amzn.to/3HiUMcK

Female Entrepreneur's Playbook: Secret Strategies From 20+ Women for Building a Business You Love and Getting Paid for It
https://amzn.to/3kqnKNO

Mind Your Business: A Workbook to Grow Your Creative Passion Into a Full-time Gig
https://amzn.to/3oqm4oV

Small Business For Dummies
https://amzn.to/3F79Wjd

Everyone Is an Expert

Whether you currently work in a cubicle, an auto shop, or behind a restaurant counter, always remember there is something that you are very good at doing. Whether it is a talent, hobby, or passion, you are an expert at something. You know more about that thing than others. And there is likely a market out there filled with clients or customers willing to pay for your expertise. Instead of giving your talent away to an employer, put that talent and knowledge to work for yourself!

Start calling yourself an expert, and really believe it. There are plenty of people who don't know much – if anything – about whatever it is you are really good at doing. And many will pay you for your expertise.

Whatever it is you decide to do as a self-employed small business owner, you will find the most success when you apply your expertise to the things you know best. For example, Rene's most successful articles cover her favorite topics: travel, pets, small business operations, and health. Jim knows how to quickly and cost effectively build e-commerce websites after creating many of our own online stores. Both of us, however, turn to other experts for contracted services beyond our scope of understanding.

Narrow Your Niche to Succeed

You might be good at many things, but you can't be all things to all people when you're self-employed. The best odds for success align when you identify a specific unmet need within a marketplace. Then, you go deep and focus your energies on meeting that need. This is known as creating a "niche" business.

> *A business niche is a specialized or focused area of a broader market that your business serves specifically.*
> – BUSINESS NEWS DAILY
>   HOW TO FIND YOUR BUSINESS NICHE
>   HTTPS://WWW.BUSINESSNEWSDAILY.COM/6748-BUSINESS-NICHE-CHARACTERISTICS.HTML

Creating a niche business helps you stand apart from others because you are serving a very targeted marketplace. Finding success within your niche is easier than if you went after a general audience. Your marketing costs are lower because they are more focused. You'll have fewer competitors. And the customers you serve will be grateful "Zombie Loyalists" because someone met their needs. Some examples of niche businesses include:

- Dog trainers specializing in reactive dogs
- Antique appraisers specializing in model trains, clocks, etc.
- Mobile mechanic for specific RV types, like vintage Airstreams
- Open water fly fishing guide
- Handicapped / Adaptive RV remodeling
- RV driving instruction by and for women
- Colorado gravel bike tour guide

There is a niche for everyone.

Jim told this to an audience of pet bloggers when he presented a pet blogging and social media conference. Pet blogging is a niche in itself, much like "mommy blogging" or RV and food blogs. He told the room filled with bloggers "Our Tripawds website serves a very small, quite specific niche. If we can do what we've done for people with three-legged pets, you can dominate your own niche too."

This holds true for food bloggers in general, versus a blog dedicated to baking the best pie in the world, or one focused on a gluten-free diet. A blog about Airstream restoration or overland vehicle expeditions will draw a more targeted audience than the countless RVing blogs out there. Those focused on a specific niche will likely draw more traffic, and customers, specifically searching for what that site has to offer.

There's always room for number two.

Once you've narrowed down your niche, do your research to determine how saturated the market is for your product. If you find one leading resource focused on your area of expertise, figure out how to differentiate yours. On the other hand, if you find numerous websites competing in the same space, consider rethinking your business focus or narrowing your niche down even further.

For more ideas and inspiration, check out these books and articles. Then read on for details about how we grew our micro-niche business to support our nomadic lifestyle.

RECOMMENDED READING

Niche Down: How To Become Legendary By Being Different
https://amzn.to/3kl9eH4

Niche, Please!: How to Narrow Your Focus and Grow Your Small Business
https://amzn.to/3mY1oF0

Niche Ideas Untapped for Your Next Business
https://amzn.to/3H6JKHq

Who Am I Today? A Daily Journal to Help You Find Your Niche
https://amzn.to/3BYYC6U

Will It Fly?: How to Test Your Next Business Idea
https://amzn.to/3n15k82

Zombie Loyalists: Using Great Service to Create Rabid Fans
https://amzn.to/3rgDJAL

Zombie Loyalists (Book Review)
https://liveworkdream.com/2015/07/29/fulltime-rver-business-tips

How to Find Your Business Niche
https://www.businessnewsdaily.com/6748-business-niche-characteristics.html

How we discovered our niche

Talk about a "niche" business! Our first remote business idea grew organically from our dog Jerry's blog. We first created Tripawds.com in 2006 to document his positive experience as a three-legged dog. Over time we realized there was virtually no ongoing support and resources available online for people coping with their pet's amputation. Today we have a robust online community and store with infrastructure that allows Tripawds users to help each other without much oversight on our part. For example:

- We added Discussion Forums and a chat room so members could talk directly with one another instead of emailing us all their questions.
- Our most popular products include self-published e-books that are automatically delivered to the customer without us having to do anything.
- Our storefront showcases and sells helpful mobility aids for animal amputees, including harnesses, books, and nutritional supplements – all fulfilled via drop-shipping or affiliate sales
- Our gift shop features Tripawds apparel, books, and gifts produced and shipped via various print on demand providers. The only product we ship is the custom jewelry Rene makes in our mobile studio.

By automating processes as much as possible, we have more time to focus on content development and administrative needs. With the Tripawds community site running smoothly, we can focus on building other areas of income generation. For example, Rene continues to pursue her freelance writing career, while Jim offers WordPress management and design services to new and existing clients.

The reward of working from the heart is greater than we ever imagined. What began with a simple WordPress blog morphed into a community with thousands of other people walking the same path we did. All members and visitors to our site are in need of hope and inspiration during an emotionally traumatic time. We take pride in being there to support each and every one of them with factual information and helpful products for their amputee dogs and cats.

In 2019, we published our memoir telling the story about how we hit the road with Jerry. ***Be More Dog: Learning to Live in the Now*** details our many adventures during those first two years on the road with our Chief Fun Officer. The book also describes how we turned Tripawds into our full-time labor of love that still keeps us on the road today.

That's when we launched the Be More Dog website where we sell e-books, autographed books, branded apparel and Rene's custom jewelry. We also drop ship paperback books via Ingram to minimize inventory we must stock. And, we drive traffic with affiliate links for those who prefer to buy on Amazon. Jim wrote about how and why we chose to self-publish our book using both Amazon KDP and Ingram Spark in our Live Work Dream blog.

New Business Considerations

The self-employed lifestyle isn't something you clock out of at 6pm. All successful entrepreneurs eat, breathe, and live their business each and every day. If you're looking for a job that you can leave at the office, self-employment may not be for you.

Making time to earn money from something you're passionate about is easy IF you remember that you get out of it whatever you put into it. When you are in charge of the company, you're the sole person responsible for the success or failure of your business.

Do you have the passion, discipline and enthusiasm to be your own boss, from the location of your dreams?

If you're ready to get started, but feel uncertain about your capabilities, don't panic. Turn to one of the many talent marketplaces we described earlier for assistance. There are also many resources for developing the skills you'll need to succeed.

For help learning everything from web development and graphic design to marketing and small business management, check out Tuts+ on Envato. Watch numerous tutorials for popular software programs and online platforms. You'll also find many free and inexpensive online courses that can help you refine your skills or learn a new one.

What will you do for supplemental or replacement income?

If you are currently employed with a job you like, or have other revenue streams requiring your attention, then you might only be looking to supplement your existing income. Perhaps you have been laid off or are unemployed for other reasons. Or, you want to become self-employed for other reasons. In that case, you'll need to work hard enough to replace your income.

Anyone fortunate enough to already have enough monthly revenue to meet their needs can enjoy supplemental income by turning one of their purpose-driven passions into a small business.

If you're taking the leap to self-employment, it's important to maintain a steady income while ramping up your own business. For instance, when we started our first business in 1998, Rene continued working full-time while Jim stayed home growing our client base. Once he became overwhelmed with design and production work, Rene quit her job to grow the business. We've been entrepreneurs working from home ever since.

Will you grow the business full-time or part-time?

Assess your personal and future business financial needs to determine whether you can work at it part-time, or dive in full-time. Research your industry, create a budget estimating monthly expenses, then forecast your profits. These are the first steps to take before creating a business plan.

Running your own business gives you freedom to do things your way. But the phrase "be your own boss" can be misleading. Sure it sounds great, but before you make the leap to starting your own business, consider how hard your current boss works. If you are willing to work even harder, then give it a try! The ability to make your own hours is a perk of being your own boss. If your clients don't need you at certain times of the day, they don't need to know you're getting the work done after happy hour, from a hammock in the woods, or on a beach somewhere.

Does it make you want to get up in the morning?

Your business should be something that you're enthusiastic about. It should make you want to get up in the morning, and focus on growing it every day. Of course it must generate an income that supports your lifestyle and utilizes your existing (and strongest) skill sets. This makes you more likely to succeed than if you started everything from scratch.

Ideal components of your work-from-anywhere business:

▶ Be as automated as possible to allow time to enjoy life on the road

▶ Not require large amounts of inventory and equipment

▶ Be easily managed on a less-robust wireless Internet connection

▶ Easily replicated to help expand your customer base

Don't Reinvent the Wheel

Starting any new business from scratch can be expensive, time consuming and risky. The best advice we have if you want to start your own is: Don't reinvent the wheel.

Don't invest the time, money and effort required to develop your own infrastructure for product development and customer relations when there are plenty of manufacturers and platforms with systems already in place. If your potential business requires heavy equipment and carrying bulky inventory, you may want to rethink the idea. A portable, low overhead business is best suited for remote living lifestyles. Those based on providing services that can be provided remotely, or delivering information products like e-books and video, are the best.

Resources to Help with Start Up

If you still believe you have a promising business idea that will fly, and want to implement it your way but have no entrepreneurial experience, seek some professional start-up help before you quit your day job.

Find a good bookkeeper. Work with someone who understands the industry you want to pursue. And later, who can review your records throughout the year to ensure your profitability. You don't necessarily need a CPA, but working with a certified tax preparer who also oversees your bookkeeping can ensure your books are accurate and legal. You might want to have them train you on bookeeping software (we use Quickbooks Pro). Then your bookkeeper can do quarterly reviews of your Quickbooks files to check for accuracy.

When you are self-employed, you'll also discover that another benefit is the ability to write off certain expenses and take advantage of specific tax deductions available only to entrepreneurs. Everything you purchase related to running your business may help lower your taxes. This includes not only whatever materials you use, but also office supplies, utilities, rent, and perhaps even some fuel, meals, and entertainment. We work with an awesome accountant who understands our digital nomad lifestyle. When first starting our business on the road, we found helpful information and more important tax tips in George Montgomery's book, <u>Can I Write Off My RV?</u> We've also discovered the more current <u>Taxes for RV Owners 2019 Edition</u>, by federally authorized tax advisor Heather Ryan EA. Who shares, "what every full-time RVer should know about taxes."

Consult with a professional tax preparer, bookkeeper, or financial consultant to determine the tax benefits specific to your business. You can find many through the local <u>Small Business Development Center</u> (SBDC) in your area. The

SBDC team can connect you with expert consultants who will provide direction and guidance. Best of all, this service is free or on a sliding scale.

SCORE, WAHVE, and BusinessAdvising.org are three resources for finding start-up help from expert business mentors. These organizations connect retired and senior professionals with small businesses and nonprofits needing assistance and direction.

Find a qualified lawyer if your business idea involves any sort of copyright, intellectual property, or trademark registration. Make sure you can retain rights and control of your intellectual property.

MORE SELF-EMPLOYMENT RESOURCES

Find Your Local Small Business Development Center
https://americassbdc.org/find-your-sbdc/

My Wife Quit Her Job
https://mywifequitherjob.com/

Biz Ammo, Your Small Business Arsenal
https://bizammo.com/

Entrepreneur.com: Home-based Business
https://www.entrepreneur.com/topic/home-based-business

Freshbooks Accounting for Small Business
https://www.freshbooks.com/

SCORE
https://www.score.org/

Work At Home Vintage Experts
https://wahve.com/

Business Advising and Mentoring
https://businessadvising.org

RECOMMENDED READING

Entreleadership
https://amzn.to/3oh9Hv0
Dave Ramsey's book about running a small business can help you in the early planning stages with a step-by-step guide for growing your business.

48 Days to the Work You Love
https://amzn.to/3F4VPei
Dan Miller's book can help you quickly fulfill your self-employment dream. With a foreword by Dave Ramsey, this book reveals the process for discovering your calling.

Will It Fly?
https://amzn.to/3F23Wb5
If you have what you think is a great business idea, consider reading Pat Flynn's book. This detailed guide and workbook provides helpful steps for test your next business idea so you don't waste your time and money.

The Barefoot Executive: The Ultimate Guide for Being Your Own Boss
https://amzn.to/3kzOlbp

Taxes for RV Owners 2019 Edition
https://amzn.to/30m7I0i

Top Home-Based Job & Business Ideas for 2021! Best Places to Find Work at Home Jobs
https://amzn.to/3Cockky

What If It Did Work?: How to Crush the Fear Keeping You from Your Potential and Launching Your next Business
https://amzn.to/3bhePJz

The Family Liaison Office Guide to Starting a Home-Based Business
https://liveworkdream.com/usdos-selfempguide2010/

But What Should I Charge?

Knowing how much to charge for your services is a challenging decision for any entrepreneur. A simple internet search for competitors in your market should return many results for determining the going rate for your specific industry.

Below are a few articles you may find helpful in setting your own pricing structure:

Life Hacker: How Much Should I Charge for My Freelance Services?
http://lifehacker.com/5831776/how-much-should-i-charge-for-my-freelance-services

Power Home Biz: How Much Should You Charge for Your Services?
http://www.powerhomebiz.com/vol69/charge.htm

Entrepreneur Money: How to Find the Pricing Sweet Spot
http://www.entrepreneur.com/money/moneymanagement/moneymanagementcolumnistjosephbenoit/article204732.html

Establish fair rates for your services or products.

If you offer services, decide whether you will charge an hourly rate, bill on a project-by-project basis, or a combination of both. You may want to consider charging clients on a sliding scale for different levels of service, depending on the effort required.

Whether you are a speaker, contractor, or consultant, if a company sends you to a specific location, be sure to request a per diem fee. Most companies hiring on-site consultants are accustomed to paying for lodging. If you're a full-time RVer, you might have a competitive edge that includes the ability to go where the work is, and can offer lower per-diem fees since RV parks cost less than hotels.

Marketing Your New Business

With more than 25 years of marketing communications expertise, we have experience helping companies large and small get the word out about their goods and services. One long-time favorite book that's helped us is "Guerrilla Marketing" by Jay Conrad Levinson. This classic marketing handbook is filled with money-saving strategies that help small business owners compete effectively in any marketplace. Some tactics Levinson recommends include:

Know Your Mission – Create a brief mission statement that defines the purpose of your business, who your customers are, and how you will serve them. This mission statement quickly tells others what you're all about, helps guide all your marketing efforts, and keeps you focused on your goals.

Define Your USP – Develop a Unique Selling Proposition that briefly describes why clients should choose to work with you, over your competitors.

Understand Your Features and Benefits – Features are what you or your product has to offer. The benefit is what your customer or client gains. Focus on selling your benefits to save your clients the confusion of figuring out why they need your features.

Build Your Contact List – Develop a list of everyone you know who has ever used your services in the past, and anyone who you think who may need them or know someone who does. Reach out to everyone on your list and ask for referrals from those who decline. Use one of the many email marketing platforms or CRM (Customer Relations Management) systems to collect email addresses by offering a free incentive (e.g.; free download, 10 minute consulting call, etc.)

Create Business Cards – Include your USP and all contact information, including website address and social media. Never leave home without your cards and always ask for one in exchange when meeting new prospects.

Have a Handout – Create a flier or brochure with brief details about the benefits you or your product offer. Always include a specific call to action in your materials that excites readers into purchasing your product or contacting you for more information.

Advertise – Specify online and print publications in your niche market and request media kits to determine reach and ad rates. Budget accordingly and run small test ad campaigns at first with a specific call to action and tracking method.

Offer Promotions – Have a sale or offer discounts, free samples, and other incentives for new clients and customers.

Maintain a Website – Posting regularly to a blog and social media is an excellent way to share your expertise and enhance your search engine ranking. You'll also want to create an online brochure detailing your services with a specific call to action and contact form. Adding a shopping cart for direct sales is even better.

Promote Thyself – Write and submit articles to publications in your industry to share your expertise. Always include contact information in your bio. Always ask for testimonials and encourage customers to promote for you by leaving reviews on your site, Yelp, Google, and social media.

Utilize Social Media – Participate in niche market discussion forums and join Facebook or LinkedIn groups pertaining to your area of expertise. Create a company page on Facebook and LinkedIn for your business. Use these and Twitter to share tips, announcements, and related news to drive traffic to your profile and website. Be sure to promptly engage with all followers.

Be Seen – Depending on the products or services you offer, you may be able to generate quality business leads with as little as business cards and vehicle graphics. If you have vehicle signs, they should clearly indicate what you do and include your website address along with social media handle.

Once you've taken the first steps to establish your business and create an online presence, it's time to focus on building your brand and develop a following. In addition to advertising, email marketing, and traditional sales tactics, there are other important considerations creating dedicated fans and followers. Your happy customers and clients naturally form a much better marketing team than you could ever build by hiring professionals. If they love your product and the service you provide, they'll work for free by sharing their positive customer experiences with the world.

It all begins by delivering great products and solutions, but more importantly it means providing superior customer service. Remember: there's always room for number two. What will set you apart from any leader in your field is your ability to prevail when it comes to customer support. For instance, the number one threat to our [Tripawds Gear](#) store sales is Amazon. That is a huge challenge. But just try speaking with a human about which harness is best for a three-legged dog when shopping Amazon. Good luck with that! Call Tripawds, and Rene will personally walk you through choosing the best harness and how to adjust it correctly, while offering many other helpful tips and emotional support. This is how you create "[Zombie Loyalists](#)". That's the title of a great book by Peter Shankman which we strongly recommend for creating a dedicated following that organically grows your brand.

Get Expert Help

In today's fast-paced social media marketplace, we recommend teaming up with industry experts to make the most of your online endeavors. Using the talent and education marketplaces we provide, you can find experts, mentors and coaches to meet all your sales and marketing needs.

Our small business start-up hero Pat Flynn has also developed courses to help solopreneurs and new business owners. Pat delivers proven online business concepts and strategies to grow your audience and income. Check out his [Smart Passive Income](#) website for complete details, or see his list of current [SPI Courses](#). Another valuable website every small business owner should consider following is [Social Media Examiner](#).

RECOMMENDED READING
Guerilla Marketing: Easy and Inexpensive Strategies for Making Big Profits from Your Small Business
https://amzn.to/3qBOHS

Superfans: The Easy Way to Stand Out, Grow Your Tribe, and Build a Successful Business
https://amzn.to/3oye7xH

Zombie Loyalists: Using Great Service to Create Rabid Fans
https://amzn.to/3ovfloa

E-commerce – Setting Up Your Online Storefront

In this section we discuss e-commerce in general, various business models for selling online, and the different stand-alone platforms or marketplaces available for opening your shop.

> **NOTE:** If you're an established blogger using the WordPress platform, consider jumping ahead to our section about WooCommerce and other e-commerce solutions for your blog.

Use existing E-commerce Tools

If you produce your own products or would rather not partner with an existing manufacturer, you can still open a shop on the web. You won't need to invest too much time and money if you use the tools out there to sell your goods. Depending on what it is you want to sell, many existing websites offer an e-commerce infrastructure tailored to specific product offerings.

Sell Products with Drop Ship Manufacturers

One of the online stores we operate requires us to maintain relationships with several different manufacturers who drop-ship specific products we sell directly to customers. Our Tripawds Gear Shop is an excellent example of how we have successfully implemented drop-shipping arrangements with manufacturers. These mutually beneficial agreements allow us to sell mobility aids for three-legged dogs, without having to stock inventory.

For most physical goods we sell, we've negotiated a mutually-beneficial commission structure with the vendors who drop-ship directly to our customers. Drop shipping is a win for our manufacturing partners because it allows them to reach a whole new market, since we do all the sales and marketing. As for us, we get to take advantage of their product development, supply chain, shipping, and return policies.

Any drop shipping arrangement has pros and cons. For instance, we are responsible for building and managing our own online storefront, taking orders, processing payment, and managing returns. We process orders with each manufacturer, and enjoy wholesale costs. We keep all profits from our sales, but we also must intervene with any returns and exchanges. We've learned the hard way that it's best to automate as much as possible, and have clear store policies and return procedures.

Not having to stock inventory is ideal for the full-time RV lifestyle. We don't need to carry the dozens of items, sizes, and styles offered in our store. On the flip side, we have no control over each vendor's inventory management. Sudden out-of-stock items create more work on our end. But any inventory challenges we encounter are outweighed by the benefits of the relationship.

If you're thinking of entering into a drop-shipping arrangement with a manufacturer, be sure they always keep a well-stocked inventory, promptly fulfill orders, and maintain open communication about low inventory. Your reputation with customers is only as good as your vendor's ability to deliver excellent customer service.

RECOMMENDED READING
How to Start A Drop Shipping Business
https://amzn.to/3qFFcSt

Drop Shipping and E-commerce, What You Need and Where to Get It.
https://amzn.to/3oz7BHg

Dropshipping A-to-Z Guide: Dropship E-commerce Strategy to Earn $10K a Month
https://amzn.to/3cgRbh1

Dropshipping: How To Make Money Online & Build Your Dropshipping Business
https://amzn.to/3Fr1pb9

Sell Handmade Crafts to a Global Audience

If you're an artist, jeweler, or crafter, many online marketplaces exist online where you can easily advertise and sell your handmade wearables and collectibles. Turnkey online marketplaces like Etsy are geared towards low-tech artists who want uncomplicated and easy to use storefronts. While it can take great talent and effort to make this your full-time gig, selling handmade items can add a few bucks to your revenue streams. Just keep in mind that the only way to keep your craft business afloat is by making items that you know people want, and which you can easily and quickly replicate while still making a profit.

> *The products most likely to be able to support your family can be made quickly and efficiently without a loss of quality. If your craft lends itself to assembly-line manufacturing, you stand a much better chance of succeeding.*
>
> – PATRICE LEWIS, CRAFTS REPORT: CAN YOUR CRAFT BUSINESS SUPPORT A FAMILY? PART 1
> HTTPS://HANDMADE-BUSINESS.COM/FAMILYPART1/

Rene makes personalized jewelry that sells in the $35 - $150 range. It's not easily replicated, so we don't rely on her craft as a primary revenue stream. But it's an enjoyable, value-added service to our Tripawds community members and provides a creative outlet that's a change of pace from her regular computer-based work.

We sell the handcrafted jewelry and tags in a few different places online. Products in our Tripawds Etsy Store focus on Rene's metalwork. On our Tripawds Gifts site, we sell select jewelry and tags directly via our WooCommerce storefront. The store also includes branded apparel, annual calendars, and other gift items. And, using the Facebook Commerce Manager, we curate many products from all our Tripawds shops to sell on both Facebook and Instagram.

Rene's relationship with Etsy is complicated. We've been selling there since 2010. Despite their high transaction fees, we continue to use this marketplace because her jewelry is seen by a much larger audience than if we only sold through our Tripawds storefront. There's a lot to love about Etsy and much to dislike about it.

The Pros of Selling on Etsy:

- Setting up shop is easy and quick. You can create product categories, customize your shop with a banner, profile, shipping/return policies, and more.
- You'll also get a free URL for your shop based on your username, like ours: https://www.etsy.com/shop/tripawds
- Etsy has more sellers and customers than any other online marketplace for creatives.
- Sellers get free access to tutorials, classes and online help for just about any question involving making, selling or promoting your work.
- Community members and Etsy staff can usually answer any question you have within a few hours. It's a great way to connect with other like-minded people.
- And, should someone infringe on your trademarked designs – which has happened to us more than once – Etsy Legal is a free resource to sellers that gets interlopers to stop invading your space.
- If you pay for Etsy's enhanced features, you can also create a totally customized website that doesn't look like it's on Etsy, as well as advertising and other promotional tools.

The Cons of Selling on Etsy

- Etsy charges a small fee for every item you list, in addition to the transaction fee for each sale. There are also re-listing fees. Their prices are among the highest in the online crafts marketplace industry. This doesn't include the additional PayPal fee that's based on the item price. For example, a $10 item sold may result in a 50¢ transaction fee, plus the listing fee. Depending upon your cost of goods and time, this can quickly eat up your small profit margin. Fees also tend to go up periodically, there seems to be no end.

- The community of sellers is massive, and getting found within the marketplace is a big challenge. If you're creating a popular item like jewelry, you'll need to do your best to stand out. Knowing the best search engine optimization terms to use is essential. But premium accounts and those who pay for promotion receive priority placement in results. At least Etsy has many resources to help you learn the best marketing tactics.

- Etsy also allows pre-approved sellers to outsource manufacturing of their designs. This means that a crafter can design an item but have cheap labor produce it elsewhere. In turn, cost competition has become fierce. Many artists oppose this policy since it detracts from Etsy's original mission to directly connect crafters with buyers.

Not everyone who sells on Etsy is a maker. If you have a knack for finding valuable vintage items or deals on craft supplies, you can sell on Etsy as a "Supplier" or "Vintage" reseller. Many Etsy customers are looking for these items. <u>Etsy does, however, limit what you can sell.</u> As a supplier or vintage dealer, items must be 20 years or older to be considered "vintage," or distinctly commercial/handmade craft supplies.

RECOMMENDED READING & RESOURCES

The Ultimate Guide to Selling on Etsy
https://amzn.to/3wUg5MA

Selling on Etsy: 3 in 1 Master Class Box Set
https://amzn.to/3Dp2GyM

Starting an Etsy Business For Dummies
https://amzn.to/3nuq8VX

How to open an Etsy Shop
https://help.etsy.com/hc/en-us/articles/115015672808-How-to-Open-an-Etsy-Shop

Facebook Commerce Manager
https://www.Facebook.com/business/tools/commerce-manager

Open an Amazon Store

Affiliate marketers and niche bloggers can build their own online shop to sell products available on Amazon by populating their store with affiliate links. (See our upcoming section for much more information about affiliate marketing.) But the only way to open a true "Amazon Store" now is to Become an Amazon Seller.

Selling on Amazon

More than half of all products sold in Amazon stores are from independent sellers. By partnering with Amazon, you can open shop on the #1 online shopping website. With Fulfillment by Amazon (FBA) you'll leave the shipping, returns, and customer service to Amazon. And by selling on Amazon, you can reach over 200 million paid Prime members around the world. Whether you choose FBA, or decide to sell direct, Amazon has the infrastructure, systems, and processes to help build, grow, and market your online store.

Choose one of two ways to sell on Amazon

Selling on Amazon is a program that enables merchants to sell their products and inventory on Amazon.com. You can reach millions of potential customers by partnering with the world's largest online marketplace. Easily upload your product inventory using web-based tools, free desktop software, or text files. Amazon introduces your product to millions of shoppers, and helps your customers make quick and easy purchases. From your seller dashboard, you can easily manage your sales. Sellers receive order notifications via email and ship items directly to customers.

Amazon offers two plans to sellers:

1. With the Individual plan, you'll pay $0.99 every time you sell an item.
2. The Professional plan costs $39.99 per month, no matter how many items you sell.

For both plans, Amazon also collects a referral fee on each sale. This percentage of the sale varies by product category. Whatever plan you choose, Amazon settles seller accounts every two weeks and usually deposits funds into your bank within five days.

Once you're ready, let Amazon handle fulfillment for you with the FBA program. Amazon has one of the most advanced fulfillment networks in the world. Known as Fulfillment by Amazon, FBA provides access to the Amazon logistics network. Businesses send products to Amazon fulfillment centers that stock the inventory. When a customer makes a purchase, Amazon manages all the receiving, packing, shipping, customer service, and returns for those orders. The FBA program can also make products eligible for Prime shipping. For the right products, FBA can help you scale your business and reach more customers.

RECOMMENDED READING
How to Sell on Amazon for Beginners
https://amzn.to/3kSoF9U

Selling on Amazon For Dummies
https://amzn.to/3CHVdK9

Amazon Selling 101: Part-Time or Full-Time Income using FBA
https://amzn.to/3ol6zsr

Become an Amazon Seller
https://sell.amazon.com/start

How to start selling on Amazon
https://sell.amazon.com/sell

Beginner's guide to selling on Amazon
https://sell.amazon.com/beginners-guide

What is Fulfillment by Amazon?
https://sell.amazon.com/fulfillment-by-amazon

Sell Your Own Products, Crafts or Artwork

Etsy isn't the only game in town when it comes to selling your creative wares online. Many resources exist for selling your own products, crafts, or creative works. Most website builder platforms now include e-commerce functionality. Whether you create jewelry, upcycled home décor, or re-purposed purses, these platforms allow you to easily set up shop online. Each of them comes with their own learning curve. A bit of technical savvy or help from techie friends may be required to set up your shop.

The primary components of any e-commerce platform include the shopping cart, payment gateway, and credit card processing. A major benefit of using an established e-commerce platform is these integrated tools are all built-in. You also won't have to worry about regular software updates, security, and keeping your site up and running. Most offer built-in Search Engine Optimization (SEO) tools to help your site get found. And, when joining a large marketplace like Etsy, your work is exposed to thousands of visitors who may be searching for those unique gifts you offer.

You may prefer to launch your own website, rather than simply open shop on an existing marketplace. You can use powerful tools like Shopify, Wix, Squarespace, WordPress and others to get set up online quickly. Benefits include standing out as your own brand, and having a dedicated site without the distraction of your competitors in the same marketplace. But keep in mind that the marketing is then all up to you, and it may take much longer to ramp up sales.

The majority of e-commerce platforms and website builders offer some sort of free option or entry-level pricing. This is a great way to give it a try and see if it will meet your needs. Keep in mind that most will also charge extra for additional functionality. And, most platforms take a percentage of your sales and/or charge processing fees. Compare the features, pricing, and processing fees for the following popular platforms if you're looking for a quick and easy way to launch your online store.

CRAFT E-COMMERCE MARKETPLACES

Etsy: https://etsy.com/

Amazon Handmade: https://sell.amazon.com/programs/handmade

Big Cartel: https://www.bigcartel.com/

Zibbet: https://www.zibbet.com/

Bonanza: https://www.bonanza.com/

Art Fire: https://www.artfire.com/

Aftcra: https://www.aftcra.com/

StoreEnvy: https://storenvy.com/

Jane: https://jane.com/sell

Society6: https://society6.com/

Folksy: https://folksy.com/

Red Bubble: https://www.redbubble.com/

eCrater: https://www.ecrater.com/

iCraft: https://icraftgifts.com/

RECOMMENDED READING
15 Best Etsy Alternatives for Crafty Entrepreneurs in 2021
https://zyro.com/blog/etsy-alternatives/

Etsy Alternatives for Crafty Entrepreneurs
https://www.businessnewsdaily.com/5287-etsy-alternatives-handmade-sites.html

Etsy Alternatives: The 17 Best Sites For Selling Handmade Crafts
https://paperform.co/blog/etsy-alternatives/

Open Your Own Shop Online

We've been hosting our own blogs for years, using the open-source WordPress content management system. So WooCommerce is our preferred e-commerce platform. See the upcoming blogging e-commerce section for complete details about this solution for selling online. Depending upon your needs, and technical expertise, there are many other platforms available to create your own online store.

Below are details about a few leading e-commerce platforms that might be a good fit for your business. Descriptions from each website are included for your review. Refer to the list of e-commerce marketplaces and website builder platforms for additional resources

Shopify
http://shopify.com

Use Shopify to create your web store, with everything you need to start selling online quickly. You don't need to have any technical or design experience to easily create a beautiful online store. Simply choose a stylish e-commerce website design, easily customize your online store, add products, and you're pretty much ready to accept payments. Got a question? Simply ask your very own Support Guru and they'll be happy to help!

Store Envy
http://www.storenvy.com/open-a-store

Build and grow your online business with one easy platform. Easily design and launch a professional store and get discovered by millions of shoppers. Store Envy offers two ways to sell. Create a customized store that looks like your business. Or, launch your Social Marketplace store for access to millions of built-in customers. This marketplace is a simple but powerful way to get discovered by new customers.

Volusion
https://www.volusion.com

Volusion is e-commerce for everyone, with everything you need to sell online. Join more than 180,000 entrepreneurs who've trusted Volusion e-commerce software to create successful online stores. Open a successful online store with Volusion for loads of built-in features, hundreds of beautiful templates, the highest security standards, and free 24x7 live technical support.

OpenCart
http://www.opencart.com

OpenCart is the best free and open-source e-commerce platform, with everything you need to create, scale and run your online business. Open source means transparent. OpenCart comes with free downloads and updates, and zero monthly fees.

PrestaShop
https://www.prestashop.com

Create and develop your business with PrestaShop. Launch your online store right now. There's a solution to suit everyone's needs. PrestaShop is an efficient and innovative e-commerce solution with all the features you need to create an online store and grow your business.

Weebly
https://www.weebly.com

Weebly offers professional online stores for entrepreneurs. Have the freedom to launch and grow your online store wherever, whenever. All the tools you need to create a site that's unique to you without any technical expertise. Credit card transactions are processed using Square, with a card reader you can use for in-person point of purchase sales.

Adobe Commerce
https://magento.com

Adobe Commerce is powered by Magento. Adobe Commerce gives you the essential e-commerce features you need to deliver an irresistible experience at every stage of the customer journey.

ZOHO Commerce
https://www.zoho.com

Zoho Commerce contains all the tools you need to build a website, accept orders, track inventory, process payments, manage shipping, market your brand, and analyze your data.

Subbly
https://www.subbly.co

Designed specifically for subscription based products and services, Subbly helps you start your subscription business in minutes. Build your brand and website, then start selling subscriptions to anyone, wherever your customers are.

Multi-Platform E-commerce Solutions

A number of platforms enable you to distribute your goods via multiple sales channels from one marketplace account. The following are a few popular solutions you can use to sell goods both in their marketplace and on your website, or via Amazon, eBay, and other online outlets.

Ecwid
https://www.ecwid.com

Join hundreds of thousands of small businesses who trust Ecwid E-commerce to sell online. Set up your Ecwid store once to easily sync and sell across a website, social media, marketplaces like Amazon, and live in-person. Get started with one, or try them all.

SELF-EMPLOYMENT

Big Commerce
https://www.bigcommerce.com

Seamlessly list, optimize, advertise, sell and fulfill products across 100+ channels including Google, Facebook, Instagram, TikTok, Pinterest, Snap, Amazon, eBay, Walmart, and Target.

More-commerce
https://www.more-commerce.com

More-commerce elevates entrepreneurs by providing access to top-selling platforms and millions of valuable shoppers. Sell everywhere with More-commerce. When you list with us, not only do your listings go up on our owned and operated marketplaces, but you'll also get access to our extensive partner network of major brand name shopping destinations. By partnering with More-commerce, you can sell on numerous platforms including Amazon, Walmart, Facebook, eBay and more.

Website Hosting: Virtually all web hosts now provide integrated e-commerce solutions. Jim's current favorite for client sites is Hostgator. Also consider BlueHost, DreamHost and SiteGround. He is not a fan of the hosting solutions Go Daddy offers.

E-COMMERCE & WEBSITE BUILDING TOOLS

Shopify: https://shopify.com/

Squarespace: https://www.squarespace.com/

Wix: https://www.wix.com/

Duda: https://www.duda.co/

Ecwid: https://www.ecwid.com/

Square Online: https://squareup.com/us/en/online-store

Indie Made: https://www.indiemade.com/

Volusion: https://www.volusion.com/

Zyro: https://zyro.com/

Weebly: https://www.weebly.com/

Paperform: https://paperform.co/

Big Commerce: https://www.bigcommerce.com

MORE E-COMMERCE RESOURCES
How to Create A Profitable online Store
http://profitableonlinestore.com/

Maximizing E-commerce
https://maximizinge-commerce.com/

How to Start a Thriving e-commerce Business
https://woocommerce.com/posts/how-to-start-a-thriving-e-commerce-business/

Be Creative: Sell Your Designs Online

Even if you're not a professional graphic designer, you can sell your designs on merchandise ranging from t-shirts and mugs to caps, calendars and more. It helps if you know something about graphic design, but most creative marketplaces make it easy for anyone to emblazon promotional materials with logos, slogans and photos.

Most storefronts have a basic shop for novice users as well as a premium store with more bells and whistles for the advanced user. Shopkeepers can choose from a huge selection of merchandise on which to have their design printed. After creating your items, you can set the selling price and your commission, and even purchase your own designs at base cost.

Creative marketplaces make opening and running a gift shop simple. Most require no up-front costs, an provide access to products you can customize with your designs. All eliminate the need to stock any inventory. Sell all sorts of apparel, mugs, stickers, greeting cards and more, letting the marketplace handle all production, fulfillment, payment processing, and returns.

First you customize the look of your shop. Then you upload your designs and select which products will feature your designs. The platform does the rest, including listing your item in their marketplace, and providing SEO settings to improve your search results.

Shopkeepers receive royalty payments for all sales and many platforms offer bonus programs. You won't make a killer income from these items, but you can set your own profit margin for each one. It's a nice revenue stream if you regularly market it to your audience.

When a customer buys an item with your design, the company produces it using high quality print-on-demand technology. They handle all payment transactions made with credit cards & PayPal, then ship your product. What's great is they also manage all returns, exchanges, and customer service.

Below are some popular options to make money with merchandise that you customize. The following descriptions are courtesy of each company.

CafePress
https://cafepress.com

The CafePress Shops service provides an online shop where you can design, manage, and sell your own branded merchandise on your website. Set up your own branded online shop, and choose from more than 450 products to customize and sell. Earn a royalty on every sale from your shop, and make more money when you reach bonus levels. View the Tripawds CafePress Store we opened long ago and our more recent Be More Dog CafePress Store.

Zazzle
https://www.zazzle.com

View our Tripawds Zazzle Store. The folks at Zazzle are passionate about providing others with an opportunity to express themselves through customization. Designs can be printed on countless different types of products. In addition to apparel, drinkware, cards, and stickers, the Zazzle marketplace includes unique items such as skateboards, sneakers, portable speakers, ties and artwork printed on canvas. You can sell your designs online for free and earn more money when referring customers by joining Zazzle's Associate program.

SpreadShirt
https://www.spreadshirt.com

SpreadShirt offers two ways for creatives to sell their designs. Users can submit designs and earn cash every time an item including their artwork is sold. Registration is free, and once you upload your design you can set your desired commission. Or, set up your own shop, create products and attract customers. Premium membership is available with a number of enhanced features including a shop with no Spreadshirt ads, personalized invoices, and promotional incentives to increase shopping.

Printfection
https://www.printfection.com

If you have an existing brand or online following, chances are you've considered an official merchandise store. You may want to sell t-shirts and other swag, but the logistics are time consuming and complex. With Printfection, you can create a turnkey shop for free to sell t-shirts, mugs, and other promotional products to your audience.

Teespring
https://teespring.com

Create & sell t-shirts you can be proud of. Sell high-quality screen printed tees with zero upfront costs and zero risk. Teespring ships directly to buyers, you keep the profit.

Sell Your Music Online

Do you play an instrument, sing or jam with other musicians wherever you go? If so, you have a number of websites to help you make money on the road. Many platforms allow you to market and stream or sell music downloads, CDs, and vinyl records. Just create an account and sell your music online. They can even help you gain direct access to digital marketplaces like Apple Music, Amazon, Spotify and more.

CD Baby
https://www.cdbaby.com

The most revenue streams for your music: Streaming, downloads, CD & vinyl sales, YouTube monetization, sync licensing, publishing royalty collection, direct-to-fan sales, & more. Anywhere you can earn money from your music, CD Baby is getting you paid.

Bandzoogle
https://bandzoogle.com

Build a stunning band website and store in minutes. Add a store in minutes and start selling music, downloads, tickets, and band merchandise today – all without any commission on sales.

DittoMusic
https://www.dittomusic.com

Reach More Fans. Release your music to more global platforms than anywhere else. Reach fans on major streaming services including Spotify, Apple Music, Amazon, Deezer and more.

Tune Core
https://www.tunecore.com

Sell your music worldwide. Get your music on Spotify, iTunes/Apple Music, Tidal, Amazon Music, TikTok, Tencent and more. Share your music and grow your fan base and keep 100% ownership of your music to stay in control of your career.

Wix
https://wix.com

The Wix website builder platform offers numerous add-ons, including e-commerce tools. The Wix Music Player app enables musicians to stream and sell individual songs and albums.

Making Money from Your Blog

This is not an e-book about how to make money from a blog. You'll find plenty of those online. Instead, we share simple ways to build, maintain and earn income from a blog (known as "monetizing").

Every business needs a website, even a start-up. Our favorite way to do it is with the WordPress blogging platform. This web-based software makes it easy to build anything from a simple site or online portfolio, to membership community and an online storefront. Adding a blog with consistent, fresh content is an excellent way to create engagement with your readers. It also keeps the search engine bots happy so customers can find you on the web.

Content Marketing Through Blogging

Content marketing is one revenue stream that has consistently worked for us over the years. It's not the only way to monetize your blog, but it's an important tool to bring in regular income from the content you write. The most simple definition of this method is:

> *Content marketing is a strategic marketing approach focused on creating and distributing valuable, relevant, and consistent content to attract and retain a clearly defined audience – and, ultimately, to drive profitable customer action.*
>
> – CONTENT MARKETING INSTITUTE
> HTTPS://CONTENTMARKETINGINSTITUTE.COM/WHAT-IS-CONTENT-MARKETING/

First, find your niche

The first step to monetize your blog through content marketing is to ask yourself: Why am I doing this and who is it for?

Millions of blogs exist on the Internet, and it's easy to get lost in the crowd. Name any general topic such as "RVing" or "Travel" and someone is already blogging about it.

To rise above them, you'll need to narrow your niche to a specific activity or topic about which you are an expert and you're passionate about. If you've started a niche business, a regularly updated blog can be a great promotional tool.

Create your blog and plan your content marketing to focus on your niche topic. Chances are, if you enjoy that specific subject or activity, there are plenty of potential readers out there who will enjoy consuming your content.

Next, regularly publish engaging content

Readers consume content in many ways, like writing, video, audio, or graphic presentations. Search engines love written content, so we'll focus on writing.

Your niche blog will have the ingredients for success if you show both passion and expertise in your writing. Offer valuable insight and helpful resources to your audience in an engaging and exciting voice. If your blog only serves as a veiled attempt to publish affiliate links and sell ads, people will see right through it. Be genuine about a specific subject and you can develop a following of dedicated readers. Publish regularly and those readers will come to expect your material. Search engines will also find you more easily.

Blogging can potentially add a sizable chunk of income to your mix, but don't rely on it as your primary source of income. A blog is not a standalone way to earn money. It is more of a marketing tool. Sales come from integrating e-commerce, affiliate marketing, membership services, and other functionality we'll get into shortly.

Expand your reach with social media.

The growth of your blog audience and brand recognition doesn't end with blog posts. To expand your reach, you'll need to integrate your blog with your social media presence. Regularly include your blog content in your Facebook posts and all your preferred social media platforms.

Consistency is key when it comes to content marketing. For best results, develop a content calendar with topics and regular timing for your posts. Then stick to it.

WordPress and other platforms allow you to schedule posts so you can write multiple posts ahead of time. There are also various tools and platforms for automating the process of sharing your posts on social media.

We use IFTTT to automate many social shares from our blogs, and Social Bee to schedule and manage our social media presence on all platforms. We also used the Buffer platform for years.

Creative ways to market yourself and expand the reach of your blog are everywhere. Beyond Facebook, Twitter, and LinkedIn, you can create quirky videos on TikTok, or post fun photos and video stories on Instagram. Pinterest is one of our top traffic driving social platforms for Tripawds.

Social media is a great way to engage with your target audience. It can also become overwhelming and time-consuming. Keep it as simple as possible:

▶ Find your tribe, and go where your audience is. Don't try to be everything on all platforms.
▶ Create some social profiles and test a few to see which ones gain traction. If you get the most engagement from your Twitter posts, focus your efforts there. If Facebook Live videos generate good buzz for you, do more of those.
▶ Engagement and consistency are key. You must interact with those who choose to engage with you to keep them coming back. Once you've gained their trust on social media, then you can drive them to your website. Do this too soon or too aggressively, and you risk losing them for good.
▶ Post regularly and use hashtags relative to your niche. Create a social media calendar to boost your content marketing efforts.

Our Primary Niche Blog Success

We never imagined that our first blog effort in 2006 would evolve into our full-time labor of love. But by focusing on our specific niche, and consistently publishing valuable information, that's exactly what happened. It took time and lots of effort, but the little WordPress blog about our three-legged dog Jerry has grown into the Tripawds community acclaimed by veterinarians and loved by passionate pet parents around the world. Just a few years after we began, Tripawds.com became the world's largest online resource for amputee pets and their people.

Growing our niche market:

- To grow our audience, we integrated Mailchimp to create a landing page with a free download for new subscribers. We also regularly update our Tripawds profiles and company pages we've created on Facebook, Twitter, LinkedIn, Instagram, and Pinterest.
- We keep content fresh and provide value to our readers, with articles about cancer therapies, pet nutrition, exercises for three-legged pets, and helpful tips for amputee pet health.
- To build our authority, we interview veterinary experts for our Tripawd Talk Radio podcast and Tripawds Youtube channel. And we build community with discussion forums and a live chat.
- Through our Tripawds Downloads store, we automate e-book sales.
- In our Tripawds Gear shop we sell harnesses and other helpful mobility gear via drop-shipping arrangements with relevant manufacturers.
- We also sell Rene's jewelry, 3-paw patches, stickers, and other fun items in our Tripawds Gifts shop.

We built even more industry credibility when we formed the 501c3 Tripawds Foundation in 2014 and launched the

Tripawds.org blog. This nonprofit side of our Tripawds organization hosts direct assistance programs for people coping with amputation for their beloved pets.

- The website helps us manage grant applications and drive fundraising efforts, like an annual auction, virtual marathon and more.
- We host our own fundraising platform too, and publish blog posts about grant recipients, fundraising campaigns, and direct assistance programs.
- The site also has a WooCommerce store for the foundation website which offers sponsorship programs and free downloads for outreach materials.

Be More Dog Blog Expands Our Reach

In 2019, we published our memoir, *Be More Dog: Learning to Live in the Now*. That is when we launched the BeMoreDog.net blog and bookstore. We currently use this website primarily to promote and sell our book by posting excerpts, with old photos and videos of Jerry, from the many scenes we wrote about our travels together.

- The Be More Dog website features a WooCommerce store for direct book sales, and automated delivery of e-books. We also include a media page listing all our podcast appearances, and an incentive page soliciting reader reviews.

Another Niche Keeps Us Busy

You may have found your way to this book from our other niche blog, Live Work Dream. We originally conceived that site as a marketing tool to sell our home-based graphics business. Once the sale was complete and we hit the road, LiveWorkDream.com morphed into our current nomadic lifestyle website.

- This is where we document our full-time RVing adventures since leaving the default life back in 2007. Live Work Dream has a loyal following because this

blog is much more than a travelogue about RV travel. Our scope encompasses the nitty gritty of living – and making a living – on the road as non-retired people living their dream.
- We consistently publish <u>workamping updates</u>, videos, <u>product reviews</u> and other relative content every week
- And we use affiliate marketing as our primary means to monetize this niche site.

We aren't sharing these websites and links to brag. Rather, we want to illustrate the many different ways you can customize blogs by implementing e-commerce, and using content marketing to serve niche markets.

Now, think about your niche and how you might craft your content. How will you configure your blog to make it a more attractive destination for your readers? And how will you use it to reach your customers?

How to Get Started Blogging

Anyone can start a blog in minutes for little or no cost. Most web hosts offer blogging tools with easy installation. There are various platforms available for publishing a blog without the need for any special expertise. Self-hosted WordPress is our preferred Content Management System (CMS) because it offers unlimited customization and control. According to <u>2021 WordPress statistics</u>, more than 39% of all websites are powered by WordPress. And when it comes to sites built with a CMS, WordPress dominates the market with a 64% usage rate. We focus on using WordPress in this book, but there are several other popular blogging platforms available.

Blogger: https://www.blogger.com/

Create a unique and beautiful blog. It's easy and free. NOTE: A Google account is required to use Blogger.

WordPress.com: https://wordpress.com

Build a site. Sell your stuff. Start a blog. And so much more. (See next section for how this differs from WordPress.org)

Typepad: https://www.typepad.com

Share your passions with the world.

Wix: https://www.wix.com

Create a website you're proud of.

Squarespace: https://www.squarespace.com

Grow your business online. Start with free website trial.

Designed for use by novices and beginners, most of these services will require a premium upgrade to implement advanced features like a blog or e-commerce. Most free blogging platforms offer very limited customization. And some may not allow affiliate or pay-per-click advertising. Please review the terms of use before deciding.

Open Source Blogging Platforms

If you're a blogger with some technical experience and the desire to have complete control over your web presence, you'll find a number of open source publishing platforms with CMS functionality. Drupal, Joomla and WordPress.org are the leaders. Unless an installer is provided within your web hosting account, these will all require some technical knowledge about FTP access and a database management. We've been using WordPress since 2006, but it is important to understand the differences between WordPress.com and the software available at WordPress.org.

WordPress.com vs WordPress.org

As previously mentioned, WordPress.com offers free blogs for those who don't want or need customization beyond the selection of tools available to its platform users. WordPress.com is powered by the same open source publishing platform software available for download at WordPress.org. Since our last revision of this book, WordPress.com has relaxed their restrictions regarding affiliate sales for sites hosted on the platform. They still, however, have limitations on how to monetize a WordPress.com site. Starting a WordPress.com site is free and easy, but the fees required for a custom domain and other enhanced services can quickly add up.

Jim had very little experience when he first installed the WordPress.org software. But with plenty of documentation available, he quickly configured it to meet our needs. Now, most web hosts offer "one-click installation" for the core software and database configuration. With a basic WordPress site up and running on your own hosting account in minutes, you'll have complete control over your site's look and functionality.

By using WordPress.org, you'll find thousands of themes and plugins to create a totally custom blog. More than 50,000 free and premium plugins exist enabling you to build a fully functional website, online store, or membership community.

Want to quickly understand the differences between WordPress.com and WordPress.org and learn the benefits of each? Years ago, we published this detailed overview with an infographic explaining it all:

How to Choose Between Self Hosted WordPress and WordPress.com Blog Publishing
http://agreda.com/2013/03/how-to-choose-between-self-hosted-wordpress-and-wordpress-com-blog-publishing/

Content Is Key

With expanding readership comes traffic. And the more traffic you have, the more appealing your blog will become to search engines – and eventually advertisers or potential customers. Over time, blog income can grow into a respectable revenue stream. The number one way to keep this momentum going is to focus on consistently developing quality content.

Pillar Articles are the most important content on any new blog. If you're new to blogging, you may be wondering, "What's a Pillar Article?"

The Blog Mastermind course creator Yaro Starak provides a detailed definition of Pillar Articles. He also provides the Entrepreneurs Journey Insider website. Pillar Articles inform readers while drawing traffic and attracting in-bound links to the article on the site where they are published.

According to Starak, each Pillar Article performs these key functions for a blog:

1. Attracts a sudden increase in traffic when first published.
2. Defines a key term or concept, answers a commonly asked question, or provides a brief how-to tutorial.
3. Keeps drawing traffic long after the article is archived deep within your blog.
4. Provides a reason for readers to bookmark and/or subscribe to your blog.

A series of pillar articles is evergreen content that is informative and not time sensitive. Often a "how to" or tutorial article, pillar articles are usually longer in length with lots of very practical tips or advice.

Although you probably won't earn immediate income just by writing one, a pillar article will usually bring in a rush of new readers and backlinks (other sites linking to your blog). It will drive search engine traffic and continue drawing new readers in, long after it is buried in your archives.

Examples of Pillar Articles

One series of pillar articles for our Live Work Dream blog includes a three post series we wrote specifically for aspiring full-time RVers. The series is titled How to Plan, Prepare and Pay for the Full-time RVing Lifestyle. These articles include important information and tips for future nomads who are still in the research and planning phase before hitting the road. We believe even seasoned RVers can benefit from what we share in the posts.

We received such positive response to these pillar posts that we've made them available as <u>one free download</u> for convenient reading offline. Years later, these posts continue to rank high in search results for how to plan and pay for full-time RVing.

Evergreen content is also important.

Topical posts help attract new readers by covering news centered on current events in your industry. But blog posts that remain relevant long after the time you write them are known as evergreen content. And it's evergreen content that keeps new readers interested and engaged far into the future.

> One good blogging habit to practice is frequently reviewing and updating your content. Go back and edit topical posts to add links to your newer pillar articles and evergreen content.

Blog Revenue Takes Time, Be Patient

No matter how many videos you see featuring a Lamborghini driving guy bragging about making millions online, the truth is that it's rare for anyone to "get rich quick" online – especially with only a blog.

Creating steady blog revenue from standard pay-per-click and affiliate advertising campaigns takes time. Have patience and diversify your income using multiple revenue streams. This ensures you don't become disappointed early on when your commissions only add up to a few dollars a month. Slow and steady is the only way to generate income from your website. Here are more tips that can help you build your online income:

Be Consistent. Keep a regular publishing schedule that features blog posts with useful information your audience will value. Follow this up with an associated social media posting schedule to expand your reach.

Use Backlinks: Make a habit of linking back to previous posts within your blog to keep readers on your site and improve search engine indexing. It helps if those previous posts have affiliate advertising links in them too.

Study Site Stats: Regularly review your site analytics (traffic figures and visitor habits) to identify your best performing content. Focus more on whatever is working well to draw traffic or generate sales.

Practice Quality Assurance: Periodically review old posts and revise them to update broken links, massage SEO terms, or add backlinks to new content.

Offer Resources: Provide a detailed Resources page with direct links to top-ranking relative articles and information. This helps readers find the information and tools they need. In return, they refer to you as an expert. Linking to high ranking information also helps improve your search engine ranking.

Write Guest Posts: Submit articles about your area of expertise to relative websites and blogs. Reach out to other publishers and offer to write informative blog posts at no charge, in exchange for a link back to your site.

Be a Helpful Expert: Comment regularly on other related blogs, social media channels, and special interest groups (i.e.; LinkedIn, Facebook, relevant discussion forums, etc.) to attract readers. Just be careful not to spam the site. Always have something relative and helpful to say.

Ask Other Experts for Help: Admit you cannot know everything. Ask experts how to start, maintain and market your blog. The web is full of free and affordable resources for doing so. Here are just a few:

- Smart Passive Income
  http://www.smartpassiveincome.com/

- ProBlogger
  http://www.problogger.net/
- Blogging Wizard
  https://bloggingwizard.com/
- Blog Tyrant
  https://www.blogtyrant.com/
- Social Media Examiner
  https://www.socialmediaexaminer.com/
- Smart Blogger
  https://smartblogger.com/
- WP Beginner
  https://www.wpbeginner.com/

Jim has had two guest posts of his own published on ProBlogger. In them, he shares insight for entrepreneurs interested in building an online community with their blog:

- How to Build Community for Niche Site Success
  https://problogger.com/how-to-build-community-for-niche-site-success/
- Tactical Tips for Building an Online Community
  https://problogger.com/tactical-tips-for-building-an-online-community/

Create Passive Income on Your Blog

Internet business guru Pat Flynn is founder of Smart Passive Income. His website and online community is packed with resources for aspiring bloggers and online entrepreneurs. In addition to online courses, you'll find genuine tips with engaging content that can help improve your blogging expertise. It was on Pat's blog where we discovered the "passive income" label that perfectly describes what we've been doing with our own websites from the beginning.

So, what exactly is "Smart Passive Income"? In the investment world, passive income is defined as, "earnings an individual derives from some enterprise in which he or she is not actively involved." In the blogging world, one is *very* involved in creating the income generating enterprise. That's the smart part. The passive part is enjoyed when that enterprise continues to earn income without any further interaction, ever again.

In other words, you may put a lot of work into developing an income generating article or information product (e.g.; e-book or video course) for your blog. Once you implement automated delivery of that product, you'll enjoy passive income in the future that requires little or no involvement other than the occasional revisions. This book, now in it's fourth edition, is a perfect example.

Three Examples of Our Passive Income

Pillar Articles: We spent hours writing our [Live Work Dream Pillar Posts](). We monetized the articles by researching helpful relevant affiliate ads and cross-promotional links to include. Since publishing the articles, we can continue to enjoy passive income from anyone who clicks those links.

Product Reviews: Some of our best income generating evergreen content are Jim's series of [RV maintenance posts]() and the many [product reviews]() we've published at Live Work Dream. With step-by-step instructions and plenty of photos or video, these articles provide helpful information to our readers. They include specific product recommendations, installation and usage tips. By targeting effective, specific keyphrases to get found online, and using affiliate links for product sales, these articles generate ongoing passive income.

E-books: We spent nearly a year developing our first niche e-book for the Tripawds community, [*Three Legs and A Spare*](). By completely automating the book's fulfillment process, we earn passive income with every purchase. Next, we launched a second Tripawds e-book, [*Loving Life on Three Legs*](). By offering a package deal with both in The Tripawds

Library for just $24.95, we sell far more of the combo than either one of the single books at $16.95 each. We have since published our third Tripawds e-book. It's specifically about feline amputation, called _Cool Tips for Three-legged Cats_. And, we repeated the automation process when we published our memoir, _Be More Dog: Learning to Live in the Now_.

RECOMMENDED READING:
Starting a Successful Blog When You Have No Clue:
7 Steps to WordPress Bliss
https://amzn.to/3Gd8SLb

How To Start A Blog & Profit From It: A Step-By-Step Guide
https://amzn.to/3EnV9ke

How To Blog For Profit: Without Selling Your Soul
https://amzn.to/3DkDhWc

Blogging for Profit: The Complete Beginners Guide on
How to Start a Blog, Earn Passive Income, and Make Money
Working from Home
https://amzn.to/3rvbrEl

But I'm Not a Writer!

If you don't think you can write, chances are, you can convey your expertise better than those readers looking for it. Most bloggers aren't professional writers and you don't need a journalism degree to share your enthusiasm about a particular topic.

RECOMMENDED READING:
Blog Writing: Best Technique to Plan and Write Blog Posts
https://amzn.to/35SxJHe

How To Be A Writer: Exercises To Improve Blog Writing
https://amzn.to/31uV5Ap

How to Monetize Your Blog with Your Writing

Even if you lack confidence as a writer, you can use simple blog posts to build your work-from-anywhere business. Any well-written, concise material you can create helps build an audience. By consistently publishing informative content, you'll get people buying your product or service, with little cost to you other than your time.

Monetizing a blog is one of the best ways to build an ongoing revenue stream. The easiest way to start growing your blog income is to focus on developing relative content, monetized with display ads and affiliate links. Google Adsense is the most popular free advertising platform.

For example, if you've started a blog about rock climbing, you can build your blog's content with gear reviews and unusual climbing destinations. Google, and many WordPress plugins, make it easy to insert display ads in your blog sidebar or within the post. When your content focuses on a specific subject, these ads will automatically be relevant to your reader. Within that content you can also make money through affiliate advertising links for the products you review and discuss.

The Amazon Affiliates program makes it simple to generate affiliate links for any product. You can also generate Amazon search boxes to embed on your site, or ads displaying specific product selections. Other affiliate advertising platforms like Commission Junction, Share-a-Sale, and Impact Radius can also help you build revenue. These affiliate advertising companies offer thousands of ways to earn commissions on products your audience wants. The best part is that you won't carry inventory or handle orders, your affiliate advertiser does all that for you! See the Affiliate Marketing section for more information.

To become a successful blogger, your goal is to create well-balanced content that makes life better for your readers. Once your own blog content is off to a good start, consider pitching your articles to other popular blogs, online publications, and print magazines. You may only need to revise your previously published articles to create fresh, new content for editors. The more places you get published, the more opportunities you have to build an audience.

- Be sure that any publisher allows you to include a byline and link in your article.
- Always strive to get paid for your work: remember you won't make money by giving it away for free. If your content is worthwhile and helpful, people **will** pay for it.

Seek Guest Bloggers

Guest blog posts are one way to fill your blog with quality content. Ask your audience and other like-minded authors in your market segment (especially ones with high search engine rankings) to write guest blog posts. Many are willing to write guest posts in exchange for a link back to their own site. Find authors by placing a call out in your blog and social media networks. Utilizing guest blog posts can build mutually-beneficial relationships and free up some of your time for other revenue generating efforts. Just make sure that the content isn't too promotional and fits well within your blog's subject area, or you may risk alienating your readers.

Guest Blog Post Tips:

- Provide guest blog specs, such as a deadline, and ideal word count (at least 300 words but generally no more than 500 words if you are not paying). Include how much, if anything, you can pay (most people don't).
- Look for content that your readers will find interesting (for example, a dog training blogger might post a guest blog entry about training devices or specific breed behaviors).
- Keep the post interesting with photos or video (be sure to get copyrights for any media you post).
- Request exclusivity in return for publishing the post and any images submitted along with it.

- Ask the author for a one or two sentence biography, and offer to include a backlink to their site.
- Mention the benefits of writing for your blog (cite traffic stats, membership numbers, recent publicity, etc.).

Write Guest Posts for Other Blogs

The benefits of guest blogging go both ways! Posting as a guest on other blogs can expand your reach and grow your audience. As a guest blogger, you can become identified as an authority on the subject, and benefit by getting links back to your own site. Find good ranking sites related to your niche that are not in direct competition for your audience.

When offering your writing services, always prepare by fully researching the blog you are pitching. Write a pitch letter specifically crafted for the blog you are pitching. Make sure your offer is genuine and conveys that you understand the subject matter. Offer to provide something helpful for the blog's readers, and request a link in your byline. Don't just cut and paste your same pitch to multiple sites. We continually receive impersonal guest post pitches about totally unrelated subject matter from "writers" who have clearly never read our blog. These emails usually make it to the trash before we finish the first line.

Earning Blog Income with Affiliate Advertising

Your website is one of the best places to create ongoing residual income. Whether you're a travel blogger writing about your adventures or a full-fledged business selling products, you have many options for earning additional profit from your website. One way is through affiliate advertising.

Including affiliate links and ads within your content is one of the easiest and most affordable ways to make money from your blog. If you do decide to implement affiliate advertising on your blog, remember one thing: People read blogs for the content, not to be inundated with ads.

When adding affiliate advertising links to your website, you'll always walk a fine line between providing valuable content for your readers while trying to make money from your website. One way to stay on the right side of that line is by manually choosing to publish affiliate advertising links that relate directly to your content and also enhances the lives of your readers. We choose affiliate advertising programs that help us provide pertinent resources for our readers, without excessively intrusive advertising that can make us appear ingenuine.

> FTC Disclosure: Articles and product reviews here may include affiliate links to third-party websites which might earn us a small commission when items are purchased. Thank you!

It is important to display an FTC Disclosure when including affiliate links in your content.

What Is Affiliate Advertising?

In any Affiliate Advertising relationship, a publisher (the blogger) partners with an advertiser to earn commissions from sales made through advertising links placed on the publisher's website. Long-time leading affiliate marketplace Commission Junction provides the following definition of Affiliate Advertising, often referred to as Performance Marketing.

> *The publisher (also known as an Affiliate, Associate, Partner, Reseller or Content Site) is an independent party that promotes the products and services of an advertiser in exchange for a commission on sales or leads.*

Publishers display an advertiser's ads, text links, or product links on their websites, in email campaigns, or in search listings. The publisher is paid a commission by an advertiser when a consumer completes a specific action such as making a purchase (a sale) or filling out a form or subscribing to a service (both examples of a lead).

Publishers regularly promote other people's products or services on their website. They want to earn a commission for sales or leads they refer, and have a blog or website where they want to place other people's ads.

An advertiser (also called a Merchant or Retailer) is a company that sells a product or service, accepts payments, or fulfills orders online.

Advertisers partner with publishers to help promote their products and services. An advertiser can be anyone who is selling their own products or services online. They are willing to pay someone else a commission for leads or referrals. They have a shopping cart or lead collection system in place and take payment through your website.
–COMMISSION JUNCTION, HTTPS://WWW.CJ.COM

In addition to Commission Junction, there are numerous platforms that coordinate affiliate partnerships between publishers and advertisers. Each company maintains a searchable database of advertisers, products, and links that website publishers can use to earn commissions from sales generated by those links. These platforms provide tracking links and/or code snippets to include in blog posts and pages. Most provide various versions of links and product photos or graphic images to be used as display ads. Many allow publishers to create custom links to specific product pages, which is important when writing content relative to your readers.

SELF-EMPLOYMENT

Sell Other People's Products and Expertise

So, you've acknowledged that you're an expert in your field, and by starting a small business and launching your website, the world knows it too. Now you can start building relationships with other authorities in the same field.

You should be able to easily find books, e-books, courses and other materials that can enhance the lives of your audience. And, you can make additional money by selling them through affiliate networks. These affiliate marketing portals enable you to find and sell downloads, information products, and tangible goods developed by others while earning commissions for each sale.

Don't reinvent the wheel! Take advantage of the expertise others provide. Introduce related products from skilled experts to your customers in blog posts, or list them in your own store, or on a resources page within your website. Thousands of experts and marketers have already published e-books and videos on virtually any topic, and made them available for download from affiliate platforms. If you've developed your own information products, consider listing them on affiliate platforms to expand your reach.

By adding affiliate sales to your income mix, you can earn a percentage of each product sale by listing the item for download from your affiliate partner's website. The affiliate platform will manage download fulfillment, process payments, and offer a searchable database for finding more great products your audience will love.

Get Started with Affiliate Advertising

Creating an affiliate account is usually free and the platforms manage all logistics while providing detailed tracking reports. Many specialty market programs also exist for niche affiliate marketing. And if you want to increase the reach for your product or service, you can create your own affiliate program by signing up as an advertiser. There are also many WordPress plugins that allow anyone to create and manage their own specialty affiliate programs.

Fully investigate any affiliate advertising program before joining. Learn more by reading Pat Flynn's Epic Guide to Affiliate Marketing or download his free Affiliate Marketing Cheat Sheet.

AffiliateTips.com is another website that provides visitors with a complete guide on how to make money online with the best affiliate programs for merchants and publishers. This site allows bloggers to find and compare specific programs and affiliate networks.

Affiliate programs may be run in-house by a specific advertiser. And there are large affiliate networks that include numerous programs from all sorts of advertisers. We work with both.

- For Tripawds, we have established affiliate partnerships with a few merchants who manage their own programs specifically relative to our niche. For instance, one manufactures a veterinary medical recovery suit. Another publishes an at-home canine rehab program.
- At Live Work Dream we frequently select affiliate programs for products related to the content we're writing by searching various affiliate networks including Amazon, Share A Sale and Impact Radius, among others.

Popular Information Product Affiliate Platforms

The following are a few leading affiliate resources to investigate for selling information products. Descriptions are direct from each platform.

ClickBank
https://www.clickbank.com

Find tens of thousands of digital products to promote online. The ClickBank Marketplace provides instant access to a vast selection of products available for promotion. Start selling niche market e-books and specialty downloads with no contracts or waiting.

Find products of interest to your audience and post referral tracking URLs on social media and in your blog. For best results, include the affiliate links in the detailed review you write about the product. You can earn passive income from commissions (up to 75% of the sale) each time someone clicks on your link to buy the e-book or other download. Visit clickbank.com and click the Affiliates link to learn more, or visit the ClickBank Vendors page for complete details about offering your own e-book for sale through their affiliate marketplace.

E-junkie
https://www.e-junkie.com

E-junkie affiliates have access to a vast selection of merchants offering e-books, how-to videos, and other downloadable products pertaining to virtually any subject matter. Affiliates earn commissions by placing referral links on their own website, usually within reviews of the product they are selling. Clicking these links sets a cookie in the buyer's browser. Every affiliate-eligible product that buyer purchases from that seller during the life of that cookie will earn you a commission, even if they go back to the seller's site directly later without clicking through your link again. E-junkie's affiliate system is free for affiliates to use at no charge. The company forbids merchants from requiring payment or any kind of fee for their E-junkie affiliate programs.

PayLoadz
https://www.payloadz.com

PayLoadz Offers a complete digital file selling service and affiliate system. Simple setup and instant payouts makes PayLoadz a leading service for selling information products and other downloads. This system works everywhere – on your website, social media, the PayLoadz store, etc.

They provide you with simple copy and paste links and button code to implement anywhere. Downloads are tracked carefully using a complex algorithm which helps prevent download abuse and fraudulent transactions.

Skillshare
https://www.skillshare.com

Become a Skillshare affiliate to access their entire catalog and earn commission for sharing unique creative content. Skillshare partners with like-minded brand ambassadors to share new classes and content being created on Skillshare each week. You'll get a unique tracking link that you can use to share any Skillshare class through a Facebook post, on your blog, in a tweet, or however you choose!

JVZoo
https://www.jvzoo.com

Since 2011, JVZoo vendors and affiliates have worked together to sell well over 18 million product units. Free to join as an affiliate or vendor, you can sell unlimited products from a single account. JVZoo offers all the features that allow you to quickly grow your business & succeed online. The customer portal will instantly deliver digital products, and JV partners are instantly paid for each transaction, removing all confusing money division.

Rakuten
https://rakutenadvertising.com/affiliate

With Rakuten, you can access over 150,000 active publishers worldwide, with a dedicated team of network development specialists who actively identify affiliates and partner opportunities across content, influencer, loyalty and more – specifically for you. Work with the top brands across industries, from fashion to financial services and more. Whether you're a blogger, influencer, app developer or business, The Rakuten premier global publisher network has you covered.

FlexOffers
https://www.flexoffers.com/publishers

Earn exclusive commissions by promoting products and services through the FlexOffers partner marketing platform. Gain access to over 12,000 advertisers all in one marketplace. The FlexOffers network provides publishers with the latest products, promotions and online-only offers from global brands and niche advertisers alike.

Avangate Affiliate Network
https://www.avangatenetwork.com/publishers

Select best-selling software titles that align with your content, drive web traffic and build brand awareness. Grow online software sales and revenues for award-winning merchants and earn additional income from your website.

Everyone's a Coach

With the popularity of life, business, and personal coaching continually on the rise, you should be able to find existing content and programs relative to your audience. Publishing platforms like Kajabi and ClickFunnels make it easy for these experts to host their own affiliate marketing programs. If you don't find the content you're looking for in your affiliate network, search for the topic and reach out directly to inquire about an affiliate program.

Top Affiliate Product Marketing Networks

The following affiliate management platforms offer a variety of ways to connect with merchants who pay commissions each time your readers buy one of their products. Descriptions have been provided by each of the respective companies.

Amazon
https://affiliate-program.amazon.com

Amazon hosts one of the largest affiliate marketing programs in the world. The Amazon Associates Program helps content creators, publishers and bloggers monetize their website traffic. With millions of products and programs available on Amazon, associates use easy link-building tools to direct their audience to their recommendations, and earn from qualifying purchases and programs.

It's easy to advertise Amazon products by building links and banners for any product. The platform also provides code for displaying search boxes or specific product recommendations. When you add these links and banners to your web page and visitors click on them from your page, you can earn up to 15% on all purchases made during their shopping session. Commissions vary greatly depending upon product category.

Commission Junction
https://www.cj.com

Commission Junction facilitates and supports equitable, lucrative relationships between advertisers and publishers. CJ manages one of the largest, most diverse and productive publisher networks in the industry. Content, email, loyalty, search, comparison shopping and emerging market sites choose to promote themselves on CJ's platform because they know they'll find access to brands they want to partner with, and because they can trust CJ to maintain a lucrative and equitable trading environment.

Share A Sale
http://www.shareasale.com

With more than 16,550+ Merchants in the ShareASale Network, publishers have access to products applicable to virtually any niche market. You decide which merchants to promote and how to promote them, and when commissions are generated, you can see your stats in real-time. All payments are consolidated from the programs you participate in, and are paid with one check or direct deposit by ShareASale once your predetermined threshold is met.

Impact Radius
https://impact.com

Impact Radius directly connects advertisers to affiliates, so true partnerships can form. The transparent platform enables true strategic partnership between advertisers and affiliates. Campaigns perform better for all.

My Lead
https://mylead.global

A comprehensive platform for earning money via Internet. In the MyLead affiliate network, you can earn without leaving home. It is a comprehensive platform offering a variety of partner programs. You do not have to invest money or have any special skills. Join MyLead and create an account today!

LinkConnector
https://www.linkconnector.com

Establish long-term relationships with globally recognized brands. Connect with our expert Affiliate Relations Team dedicated to providing in-depth support and representation. Maximize performance with exclusive LC technologies.

MaxBounty
https://maxbounty.com/affiliates.cfm

Promote high-converting cost-per-action campaigns from hundreds of advertisers seeking your blogging, media-buying, social media, and e-mail marketing expertise.

TradeDoubler
https://www.tradedoubler.com/en/publishers

TradeDoubler is a European based digital marketing company with some of the biggest clients in the world.

ClixGalore
https://www.clixgalore.com

Turn your valuable web site traffic into money now by joining Affiliate programs and driving customers to the many thousands of Merchants using the ClixGalore Affiliate Marketing network to advertise their business.

FlexOffers
https://www.flexoffers.com

FlexOffers is a one-roof affiliate marketing solution for publishers. Our database is comprised of over 12K advertiser partnerships from over 65 networks. Partner with us to benefit from our deep advertiser relationships, experience, strategy, and our network scale as we negotiate exclusive industry payouts on your behalf.

BuySellAds
https://www.buysellads.com

BuySellAds.com is a marketplace specifically for simplifying publication of affiliate ads. It makes ad buying and selling easier than ever with thousands of advertisers actively buying ads in the BSA network each month.

MarketLeverage
https://www.marketleverage.com

MarketLeverage provides Publishers access to hundreds of top-notch advertisements designed to maximize their online profits. We have the best offer payouts, rapid payments to Publishers, and have the highest paying rewards program in the industry.

Panthera Network
https://www.pantheranetwork.com

Panthera Network is dedicated to maximizing the revenue of our publisher's advertising inventory. Here you will find all the popular offers found on the other networks, as well as exclusive, high-converting offers.

Affiliate Future
https://www.affiliatefuture.com/Publishers

Connect your website to advertisers. Making money from your website couldn't be simpler. We provide you with all the tools you need to succeed.

Specialty/Niche Affiliate Marketplaces

There are also a number of affiliate platforms dedicated to connecting advertisers with bloggers publishing content related to a specific niche. Searching for "affiliates" plus keywords related to your blog will likely find more.

Market Health
https://www.markethealth.com

The Leading Health and Beauty Affiliate Program since 1998. The Market Health Affiliate Program allows you to market and promote the world's leading health and beauty offers online. We offer the highest paying affiliate program and best tracking software in our industry.

Fintel Connect
https://www.fintelconnect.com/publishers

We're publisher-first and the only affiliate platform that focuses on the financial industry. We invest in growing and nurturing partnerships, no matter how big or small.

PartnerStack
https://partnerstack.com/marketplace

The best place to promote and discover SaaS partner programs. Find affiliate partners for software, B2B brands, and cloud based SaaS (Software as a Service) solutions.

Create Your Own Affiliate Program

In addition to the affiliate partner networks listed above, there are many platforms and plugins that allow you to host your own affiliate program. This is how you turn your customers into ambassadors for your products and services. If you offer your readers an easy way to earn commissions, they will create content that promotes your products on their website and social media channels.

Check out these affiliate platforms, and plugins for hosting a program from your WordPress dashboard.

Referral Candy
https://www.referralcandy.com

Grow your sales through word-of-mouth marketing. Reward your customers for referrals and watch the sales and shares roll in.

Refersion
https://www.refersion.com

Refersion makes it easy to recruit, track, and pay affiliates. All Refersion customers also get access to a marketplace with over 5,000 potential partners to take advantage of your offer.

LeadDyno
https://www.leaddyno.com

Everything to launch & grow your affiliate program. Increase the revenue of your e-Commerce store or SaaS business. Quickly and easily set up our all in one affiliate tracking solution.

Ambassador
https://www.getambassador.com

Ambassador helps you dramatically increase your revenues and reach by turning your happiest customers into a virtual army of brand advocates.

UpPromote
https://uppromote.com

Build, manage, and succeed with affiliate marketing. Tell your brand's story with ambassadors' voices. Let real-time tracking and powerful affiliate management software grow your Shopify business.

Post Affiliate Pro
https://www.postaffiliatepro.com

Manage multiple affiliate programs, track affiliate partner performance, assign commissions and issue payouts on one platform.

Podia
https://www.podia.com/

Everything you need to sell courses, webinars, downloads, and community.

Affiliate Program WordPress Plugins

Plugins are optional add-ons that can be installed to extend the functionality of any WordPress website. Many plugins exist for managing your own affiliate marketing program. Most feature e-commerce, membership, and marketing integrations that connect with MemberPress, WooCommerce, PayPal, Stripe, Mailchimp and more.

- Easy Affiliate:
  https://easyaffiliate.com
- AffiliateWP:
  https://affiliatewp.com
- WP Affiliate Manager:
  https://wpaffiliatemanager.com
- Affiliate For WooCommerce:
  https://woocommerce.com/products/affiliate-for-woocommerce
- Solid Affiliate:
  https://solidaffiliate.com

- Affiliates:
  https://wordpress.org/plugins/affiliates
- WordPress Affiliates:
  https://wordpress.org/plugins/slicewp
- WP Affiliates Manager:
  https://wordpress.org/plugins/affiliates-manager

RECOMMENDED READING

Affiliate Marketing For Dummies
https://amzn.to/3pHfVVS

Affiliate Marketing For Beginners 2021: Make A Six-Figures Income From Home
https://amzn.to/3oL4bSO

Pat Flynn's Epic Guide to Affiliate Marketing
https://pages.smartpassiveincome.com/epic-affiliate-marketing/

Pat Flynn's Affiliate Marketing Cheat Sheet
https://www.smartpassiveincome.com/affiliate-marketing-smart-way/

How to find the Best Affiliate Network
https://www.affiliatetips.com/find-best-affiliate-networks/

Earn More Blog Income from Pay Per Click Advertising

Pay-per-Click (PPC) advertising generates income by directing direct search engine traffic to websites, in exchange for a small commission from the advertisers. These advertisers pay publishers a small commission whenever their ad is clicked, whether or not a customer actually buys a product.

If you want to publish pay-per-click ads on your website or blog, consider the most widely used PPC campaign program, Google AdSense. This is an easy way to earn money from your online content. All you need to do is use the code provided to display relevant, engaging Google ads on your site.

Google offers a number of ways to earn revenue with AdSense ads.

AdSense for Content

Google AdSense provides a way for publishers to earn money from their online content. Display targeted ads on your website using Adsense content ads and earn revenue from valid clicks or impressions. (An impression is any time the ad appears on your website.) AdSense works by matching ads to your site based on your content and visitors. The ads are created and paid for by advertisers who want to promote their products. Since these advertisers pay different prices for different ads, the amount you earn will vary.

AdSense for Search

AdSense for Search lets you offer your users the ability to search Google directly from your posts and pages. By placing an AdSense for Search box on your site, you'll generate earnings from ad clicks made by users on the search results pages.

You won't, however, receive revenue from searches performed through your AdSense for Search box. You will only earn revenue when users click ads within the search results. If users perform searches on your site, but choose not to click any ads on the search results pages, you will not receive any earnings.

If video is a major component of your content strategy, consider reviewing the YouTube Partner Program eligibility requirements.

AdSense for Games

If you are a web-based game developer, Google's H5 Games Ads is a program – currently in beta mode – which may allow you to earn revenue by showing interstitial and rewarded ads in your HTML5 (H5) browser based games. Learn more about H5 Games Ads (beta).

Google Admob

Google no longer supports integration of AdSense ads within mobile device apps. If you are an app developer, you can now earn more revenue with your apps using the Google Admob program. You work hard on your app. AdMob makes earning revenue easy with in-app ads, actionable insights, and powerful, easy-to-use tools that grow your app business.

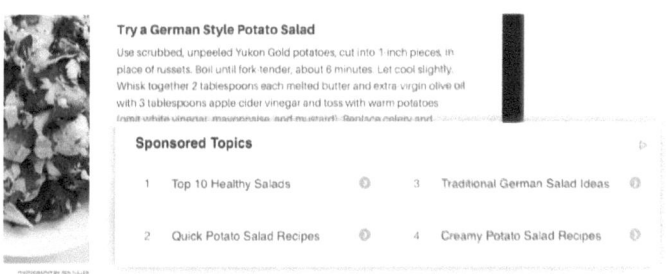

Contextual Advertising displays relative text link ads to your readers.

Sell Text Link Ads

Many bloggers sell text link advertisements on their website as part of their income strategy. When your blog rises in search engine rankings, you may receive requests by businesses who want to buy text link ads on your site. If you want to take them up on it, be prepared to respond with several types of ad sizes, placements and price ranges. Establish your advertising guidelines and pricing ahead of time so you can respond quickly to these requests. For example, you may choose to offer display ads in your sidebar, or text links within your content.

For our two primary niche blogs Live Work Dream and Tripawds, we now only offer text link ads on the home page of each site. We've established a monthly rate, and offer six or twelve month contacts, with a reduced rate for renewing. Sending an email and leaving the ad in place, is less work than removing the ad when it expires. We closely review all potential advertisers for relevancy, as well as the text links and anchor text they request. We also provide a discounted rate for longer term ads, or if an advertiser chooses placement on both sites. We also offer renewal discounts.

If you decide to pursue direct sales with advertisers, you can see ongoing income from renewals of the ads. As long as the customer is happy with the amount of traffic generated to their site from those links on your site, they'll come back and renew. If you have a high ranking site, some ad agencies may be interested in placing text ads solely for the backlink from your site. In this case, you may get away with placing links in a discreet location on your site like we do. We only include text link ads in a specified "Sponsored Links" section near the bottom of our home pages.

If you're considering selling ads directly, but don't know where to begin or what to charge, consider checking out the following resources.

RECOMMENDED READING
The Ultimate Guide to Ad Sales: How to Sell Ads Directly
https://monetizepros.com/ad-sales/guide-to-ad-sales/

How Much Should I Charge for my Advertising Space?
https://problogger.com/how-much-should-i-charge-for-my-advertising-space/

Selling Text Links
https://problogger.com/selling-text-links/

Moz SEO Blog: Our Stance on Paid Links & Link Ads
https://moz.com/blog/our-stance-on-paid-links-link-ads

Making money from blog text link ads can take time if you don't have a large readership, high page ranking, lots of readers or a huge number of social media followers. Learning how to solicit advertisers and develop partnerships can be challenging. Until then, your time may be better spent focusing on your content development and affiliate marketing efforts.

The easiest solution for text link advertising is to partner with a company that specializes in coordinating the placement of links and processing payments. In our blogs' early days, we partnered with Media Whiz (formerly Matomy SEO). This platform automates the process of placing text advertisements on our sites. They offer a simple solution for automatically embedding affiliate links within the content of articles, or publishing specific text link ads. TextLinks.net (formerly LinkAdage), and BackLinks4U, are other platforms to consider.

Stay Current on Text Link Advertising

Buying and selling text links has become an increasingly contentious, thorny issue among SEO experts. As algorithms have evolved, search engine ranking may be impaired by linking to less reputable sites. For more information, read how leading SEO industry experts at Moz has changed their stance on paid links.

TEXT LINK AD PLATFORMS

Media Whiz: https://www.text-link-ads.com/

TextLinks.net: https://textlinks.net

BackLinks4U: https://www.backlinks4u.com/

Media.net: https://www.media.net/

Vibrant: https://www.vibrantmedia.com/

PopAds: https://www.popads.net/

Sovrn: https://www.sovrn.com

Infolinks: https://www.infolinks.com/

Develop Brand Engagement Relationships

Instead of making a few cents here and there with affiliate ads and text links, consider developing direct relationships with brands to engage with your audience. Custom tailored marketing campaigns can generate thousands of dollars in exchange for unique online marketing and social networking engagement that might include:

- Offers to produce co-branded multimedia and product review videos.
- Publishing sponsored articles and give-aways
- Host dedicated internet radio shows and podcasts.
- Expand your influence, and your income, by incorporating live speaking engagements, event marketing, social media outreach and more into your brand engagement opportunities.

Over the last few years we traded site-wide banner advertising on our main Tripawds blog for the opportunity to have brands engage with our community through custom tailored multi-faceted partner campaigns. These might include publishing sponsored content, producing a product review video, and/or hosting a podcast interview in addition to strategically placing image or text link ads throughout the website.

If you plan to offer relationship marketing opportunities on your blog, it's important to create a landing page for potential partners that includes:

- Detailed information about your target audience and the content you regularly publish or services you provide.
- The benefits your partners/sponsors will receive by aligning with your brand.
- Demographics and statistics.

Save any fine details and discussion about compensation rates for further direct communication via email or telephone. Once you and your potential partner come to an understanding about a mutually beneficial arrangement, you can then develop a proposal and action plan. As an example, you can review our <u>Tripawds Brand Engagement Opportunities</u> page.

WordPress E-commerce: Set Up Your Blog Shop

We began our e-commerce strategy when we implemented many of the revenue generating tactics discussed in the previous pages. Here's how it has evolved:

1. First, we set up our Adsense advertising account with Google and added banner ads and text links.
2. Next we added affiliate advertising from our accounts with Amazon, Commission Junction, Clickbank, and Share-a-Sale.
3. Then we developed our content marketing by writing useful content for our blogs, and researched appropriate affiliate links for products readers would find useful.
4. Next, we started working directly with brand partners by creating custom campaigns including advertising, sponsored content, and audio/visual media.
5. Finally, we launched our online stores to sell products directly and via affiliate links.

As our blog content grew, so did our traffic. To boost our revenue, we first installed a PayPal shopping cart. This allowed us to sell products via our relationships with partners who drop ship products to our customers. As better e-commerce tools became available for WordPress, we upgraded our sites to enhance our online storefront capabilities.

<u>WooCommerce</u> is now our preferred e-commerce platform. This platform integrates seamlessly with WordPress, meets all our needs, and has incredible customization capability. If you don't use WordPress, or want to review other options, please refer to our previously listed resources for other solutions to create your own online shop.

WooCommerce is the leading shopping cart plugin, developed and supported by AutoMattic, the same company that maintains WordPress. So you know it will always integrate seamlessly with the core software.

Why WooCommerce?

- It is ideal for selling tangible goods, services, or digital downloads.
- The free plugin is fully functional for quickly launching any basic online store.
- It provides the ability to create various product types with full shipping and inventory management.
- Allows customization of shipping options, coupons, sale pricing, unlimited product variations, multiple payment gateways, and much more.
- Wizard style set-up enables quick and easy configuration of sales tax and shipping options.
- Numerous premium WooCommerce add-ons and third party plugins are available for customizing your shop to meet your needs.
- With annual subscriptions for premium features, you can use WooCommerce to sell memberships, subscription plans, events, web-based courses, and much more.

If you're not certain where to begin selling online, regardless of which platform you plan to use, read this comprehensive overview for complete details about setting up your e-commerce business – and using WooCommerce:

How to Start a Thriving e-commerce Business
https://woocommerce.com/posts/how-to-start-a-thriving-e-commerce-business/

Popular E-commerce Solutions for WordPress

As we mentioned earlier, most website hosts provide an integrated e-commerce solution. Many offer simple wizard-based installation of WordPress and WooCommerce. For information about other platforms, refer to our previous section and Resources list for e-commerce marketplaces and other platforms.

Since publishing our first edition of this book, and the acquisition of WooCommerce by the WordPress parent company Auttomattic, numerous e-commerce plugins for WordPress are no longer developed nor supported. The following are a few remaining shopping cart plugins which Jim has direct experience using, either for us or his website clients. Others he has reviewed, or found worthy enough to include here:

WooCommerce
https://woocommerce.com

Build exactly the e-commerce website you want. WooCommerce is a customizable, open-source e-commerce platform built on WordPress. Get started quickly and add features to meet your needs.

WP eStore & eMember
https://www.tipsandtricks-hq.com/products

Use WP eStore to Sell digital and non-digital products from your WordPress blog securely. WP eMember is a robust membership management plugin for your WordPress site.

S2Member
https://s2member.com

The s2Member Framework integrates with various payment gateways, fully supports recurring billing, and provides powerful membership capabilities with protection of members-only content.

Easy Digital Downloads
https://wordpress.org/plugins/easy-digital-downloads

If you only plan to sell information products With WordPress, consider Easy Digital Downloads for e-books, PDF files, and more. Easy Digital Downloads is trusted by over 50,000 smart website owners.

WordPress Simple PayPal Shopping Cart
https://wordpress.org/plugins/wordpress-simple-paypal-shopping-cart

Easy to use free WordPress Paypal shopping cart plugin for beginners. Set up a simple shop for selling products online in one click from your WordPress site.

Ecwid E-commerce Shopping Cart
https://wordpress.org/plugins/ecwid-shopping-cart

Free plugin that integrates with your Ecwid e-commerce account. Get your online store up and running at zero cost. As your online shop grows, Ecwid grows with you.

WP Shopify
https://wordpress.org/plugins/wpshopify

WP Shopify allows you to sell your Shopify products on any WordPress site. Your store data is synced as custom post types giving you the ability to utilize the full power of native WordPress functionality.

NOTE: Before considering any free e-commerce solution, remember – you get what you pay for! Switching shopping cart platforms is a major hassle. If you have many products in your store, it's often easier to start over from scratch. So consider selecting the best platform to meet your future needs, from the beginning. In our opinion, that's WooCommerce! And no, we don't work for Woo and we have no affiliate arrangement. Jim is just a Zombie Loyalist.

Blogs, Vlogs, and Podcasts

Any current discussion about blogging and making money online would not be complete without mentioning video and podcasts. Perhaps writing is not your thing. If you like speaking your mind or feel comfortable in front of the camera, starting a video channel or podcast may be more your style. We still recommend you create a website and start a blog. If you ever hope to attract notable guests or sponsors onto your show, you need a website providing details about your audience and contact information. Even if you only publish your audio/visual content on their platforms, there are simple ways to syndicate that content through your blog to keep it archived on your site.

Video Blogging (Vlogging)

YouTube is the leading platform for hosting Vlog (Video Blog) episodes. Starting a YouTube channel is quick, easy, and a must if you ever plan to monetize your videos. We know acclaimed niche experts who only use social media for vlogging. But publishing your video content on your website, along with transcripts or other value added copy, is a great way to keep search bots finding your content. Video can also become an integrated component of your content marketing strategy. To directly monetize your videos, you must meet the [YouTube Partner Program](#) eligibility requirements.

Why Become a Podcast Host?

If you want to make money podcasting, you better be prepared to work hard, and be patient. Yes, there are podcast hosts making good money. But the industry is incredibly saturated and competition is tough – especially for any new podcast. As we've mentioned before, the best first step is to narrow down your niche and identify your target listener. Then consistently produce high-quality relative content for that specific audience.

Without a large existing following or big celebrity name, you are not likely to have a successful general topic podcast. And there is already a podcast about everything, so you better refine your focus and stick to that format. It is important to have good recording equipment, but you don't need to break the bank for the basics.

How and Why We Podcast

Our [Tripawd Talk Radio](#) is unlike most podcasts. Our special interest topic is targeted at a very specific audience. And, we do not publish new episodes on a regular schedule. The podcast, however, is an integral part of our blogging content strategy. Our show has a Q&A format, with Rene interviewing leading veterinary experts, oncologists, surgeons, and rehab therapists.

We sometimes publish our episodes weeks or even months after the interview. This allows us time to produce the audio and video version. We also get the show transcribed and publish the full transcription along with additional commentary and resources. This creates excellent evergreen content, and provides readers the option to consume our content in their preferred format.

Want to get started podcasting? Read Pat Flynn's free How to Start a Podcast tutorial. This covers all the basics from why you should start a podcast and the equipment you need, to choosing a podcast host and producing your first episode. He also offers an advanced course, Power-Up Podcasting – a step-by-step course to launch a successful podcast that gets found and grows your online brand.

Like any website, every podcast needs a hosting provider. This platform is where you'll upload your episodes that will be distributed to all the popular podcast listening apps. After hosting our show on BlogTalkRadio for years, we tired of their advertising and poor support. We now use and recommend BuzzSprout. This platform offers everything the beginner podcaster needs to launch a show and is very affordable.

You can **try BuzzSprout for free**, and paid plans start at $12 per month. Get a $20 gift card for signing up at: **https://tri.pet/trybuzz20**

RECOMMENDED READING:
So You Want to Vlog?
https://amzn.to/3lToAgx

How To Start a YouTube Channel for Fun & Profit
https://amzn.to/3p0TdbW

Pat Flynn: How to Start a Podcast
https://www.smartpassiveincome.com/guide/how-to-start-a-podcast-tutorial-pat-flynn/

Podcasting for Beginners Value Edition
https://amzn.to/3F7kH5G

So You Want to Start a Podcast
https://amzn.to/3IQxqfd

Profit from Your Expertise

As we've mentioned before, everyone's an expert about something. By implementing the business strategies we've already presented, you can launch your own niche online business posed for growth while working from anywhere. With your knowledge, a little charisma, and solid business sense, you can be a successful coach attracting clients seeking your guidance. There are now <u>coaches for everything</u>.

What Is A Coach?

A coach is like a mirror that reflects your ambitions and potential. When you try to achieve something new, you want someone with you on the journey. Think of a coach as a guide who takes you from where you are now to where you want to be. This could be a mentor, a teacher, or just **a person you share ideas with**.

Why Should You Become A Coach?

Being a coach is not an easy job, but it's not impossible either. Imagine being the person responsible for the other person to achieve their goals and dreams. Imagine being a conduit through which someone can be the person they want to become.

<u>CoachFoundation.com</u> says, consider becoming a coach if:

- ▶ You are the kind of person who loves to have this kind of responsibility.
- ▶ You get satisfaction from giving yourself over completely to the service and happiness of others.
- ▶ You love seeing the look of gratitude on your client's face.

Self-publishing and public speaking are other ways to profit from your expertise. With adequate writing skills, you can become a published author using any self-publishing platforms. If you're also good at public speaking, you might market yourself for motivational or educational speaking engagements. Or you might focus on producing audiovisual content for your YouTube channel or podcast. Whatever path you choose, if you plan to grow your business online, consider creating a community for your customers, clients, fans, and followers.

RECOMMENDED READING

How to Become A Life Coach and Build a Thriving Practice
https://amzn.to/3e0VCNQ

Make Money As A Life Coach
https://amzn.to/3IZ9vdm

31 Types Of Coaching – A Complete List (2021)
https://www.coaching-online.org/types-of-coaching/

THE 10 TYPES OF COACHING (+183 Subtypes) Categorized
https://www.coaching-online.org/types-of-coaching/

Create and Sell Online Courses
https://www.smartpassiveincome.com/learn/online-courses/

Build Your Community, Grow Your Business

Whether you're a business, life, or personal development coach offering courses and consultation services, or a niche expert selling information products, one of the best ways to grow your business is to build an online community. Many people use private Facebook groups for this purpose, but we do not consider this a suitable niche membership community platform. Here's why:

- ▶ Facebook users are constantly bombarded by a steady stream of distraction and unrelated, often competitive, advertising.
- ▶ Group discussion takes the form of continuous stream, solely organized by the most recent comments. Search functionality is very limited, making

- it difficult to search specific information. And the endless stream of unrelated comments and duplicate information lacks decent archivability.
- Unless properly moderated, Facebook groups frequently turn ugly with spam and divisive content from trolls and opinionated users. We speak from experience here, having managed the <u>Workampers Facebook Group</u> for years which has grown to 60,000+ users.

The most popular and successful online communities are found on niche websites, not social media. These often feature discussion forums and other social tools that foster safe engagement among members regarding a specific subject. Community aspects of the site are often free, and provided in addition to the primary content published and products offered on the website. Or, websites of coaches and other entrepreneurs may feature a community delivering protected content only to paid members. Tiered membership plans may enable access to different levels of content and/or one on one coaching.

How We Built Our Niche Community

With Tripawds, we have created a niche online community of passionate pet parents helping each other through amputation recovery and care for their beloved pets. We provide all community features free of charge. These include popular discussion forums, a live chat room, private messaging, and member blogs with access to endless blog design themes and plugins for sharing their stories.

Explosive growth of the Tripawds network – and our business – began when we first installed the forums in 2008. Since then, we have archived 17,000+ topics with hundreds of thousands of searchable forum posts. Jim launched our blog network in 2009, and we now host more than 1,900 three-legged dog and cat blogs. Our community has currently grown to 19,000 registered members with more joining every day. In <u>our many podcast interviews</u>, we always attribute the success and reach of Tripawds to the power of our community.

Making Money with Free Services?

We operate Tripawds on the "Freemium" business model. The website offers free support and services, and we consistently publish informative public content. Anyone can create a user account with access to all community features, and start a free blog. For a nominal fee, members can pay for premium functionality including instant removal of ads on their blog and access to additional plugins. For those who want to save time searching all our free content, we offer various e-books for fast answers to common concerns.

> For a funny story about how we stumbled upon our business model, read an excerpt from our *__Be More Dog__* book in which Jim explains the freemium model: https://bemoredog.net/freemium-business-model

We built Tripawds on a WordPress multisite network with numerous plugins to integrate discussion forums, live chat and other community-building features. This created a full-time job for Jim as our administrator.

Today, you'll find numerous fully integrated platforms designed specifically for building a robust online community. Most platforms incorporate community features, members-only content protection, email marketing, and more. Many feature customer relationship management (CRM) tools, in addition to standard website / landing page creation and e-commerce solutions. You'll also find dozens of standalone discussion forum solutions, and WordPress plugins.

The following is a list of leading resources for building a robust online community.

ONLINE COMMUNITY BUILDING PLATFORMS

Hivebrite
https://hivebrite.com
A powerful online community platform, Hivebrite provides top organizations with all the tools they need to build, manage, and engage their community.

Ning
https://www.ning.com
Create your own social network with a customized community management and social media integration.

Mighty Networks
https://www.mightynetworks.com
Build a business powered by community. Build online courses, run events, and charge for access all in your very own Mighty Network.

Circle
https://circle.so
The all-in-one community platform for creators & brands.

Tribe
https://tribe.so
A customizable community platform for businesses. Behind every successful company is the ability to engage and delight customers. Tribe enables you to do just that.

Insided
https://www.insided.com
Improve retention, customer growth, and advocacy with the all-in-one customer success engagement platform.

Kajabi
https://kajabi.com
Everything you need in a single platform. Products, websites, landing pages, payments, analytics, marketing automations, email, communities, and more.

Patreon
https://www.patreon.com
Let your fans become active participants in the work they love by offering them a monthly membership, for access to exclusive content, community, and insight into your creative process.

PeerBoard
https://peerboard.com
Everything you need to share knowledge, increase engagement, and create deeper connections with your online audience.

Disciple
https://www.disciplemedia.com
Bring your people, memberships, and content together in your own fully-branded and private community platform. Sell courses, charge subscriptions, live stream and so much more.

Participate
https://www.participate.com
Build an online learning ecosystem that inspires your members to engage and propels your impact forward.

Socio
https://socio.events
Socio is the all-in-one event platform that powers continuous engagement to drive better results for virtual, in-person, and hybrid events.

Muut
https://muut.com
Muut powers lively discussions for millions of sites, making users happier and more likely to return, with integrated forums, commenting and messaging.

Zapnito
https://zapnito.com
Zapnito is the community software platform built to showcase expertise. Build your own branded community and engage the people who really matter to your business.

Honeycommb
https://www.honeycommb.com
Give your audience, organization or community of any size their own online, modern, social space. Launch iOS, Android and web apps with minimal cost, effort & time.

SocioHub
https://www.sociohub.io
Online platform to build your branded private community. A fully customizable community management software that helps you engage, grow and monetize your community.

Brilliant Directories
https://www.brilliantdirectories.com
Monetize your community with your own online directory. Select a directory theme to launch your membership website for any industry or local area.

DISCUSSION FORUM SOFTWARE/PLATFORMS

MyBB
https://mybb.com
MyBB is the free and open source forum software powering thousands of engaging, vibrant, and unique communities across the internet.

Plush Forums
https://plushforums.com
The easy way to build a great community. With the most polished, user-friendly forum software ever.

Vanilla Forums
https://vanillaforums.com
Community software that facilities collaboration between brand and customer to build loyalty, improve support and boost engagement.

Discourse
https://www.discourse.org
Managed forum hosting to provide civilized discussion for your community.

vBulletin
https://www.vbulletin.com
Build community websites with integrated forums and blog features using vBulletin. The software facilitates content creation and discovery with simplified site management.

WORDPRESS DISCUSSION FORUM PLUGINS

Simple-Press
https://simple-press.com
The ultimate forums plugin for WordPress with enterprise class features! See our example at https://tripawds.com/forums

bbPress
https://bbpress.org
bbPress is forum software from the creators of WordPress. Quickly setup a place for discussion, subscriptions, and more!

BuddyPress
https://buddypress.org
Fun & flexible software for online communities, teams, and groups. BuddyPress helps you build any kind of community website using WordPress.

BuddyBoss
https://www.buddyboss.com
Sell memberships, courses, and build online communities. Built on WordPress, giving you the flexibility, control and freedom you need, to create a successful online platform.

Peepso
https://www.peepso.com
PeepSo is a super-light, free, social network plugin for WordPress that allows you to quickly and effortlessly add a social network or an online community, right inside your WordPress site.

WP Foro
https://wordpress.org/plugins/wpforo
Full-fledged yet easy and light forum solution for your WordPress website. This free WordPress forum plugin brings everything you need to run an efficient and professional community.

ForumEngine (Theme)
https://www.enginethemes.com/themes/forumengine
Build your online community without worries it would be abandoned. ForumEngine is optimized for a more social interaction.

Sales Funnels and Landing Pages

One of the most popular ways coaches and information marketers attract clients and sell their products are by using a sales funnel and landing pages. Simply put, a landing page is a single point of entry with a specific purpose. Usually this page promotes a specific product with a very clear call to action. Oftentimes, the landing page is part of a sales funnel designed to convert leads into loyal customers. In either case, the landing page is not a comprehensive website, but a standalone sales and marketing tool. It is designed with a specific conversion or sale in mind. Landing pages differ greatly from the home page of your website which may incorporate your additional content, blog, storefront, and more.

What is the difference between a website and a sales funnel? Your sales funnel may be hosted on your website, but it is not in itself an actual complete site with any additional content. The sales funnel serves a specific purpose. It often features a standalone landing page, or series of pages designed solely for marketing, and product sales, or onboarding new clients. The funnel concept allows you to guide your visitors step-by-step through your entire sales process.

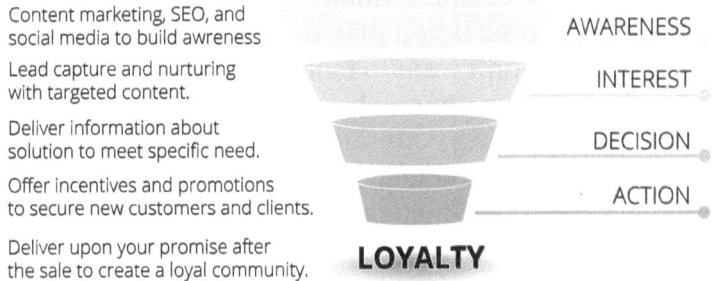

A properly crafted sales funnel can develop brand awareness, convert leads, and create loyal customers.

With a sales funnel, you determine what the potential customer sees, and in what order. This is designed so your prospects don't get confused or lost, and leave your site. The typical use of a sales funnel is to lead your customer directly to the one specific product or service they need most to help solve their problem. It provides opportunities for up-selling more valuable offerings. And the sales funnel integrates a method for following up with your visitors, even after they leave your page!

Sales Funnels integrate with email marketing services to capture the email address of anyone interested. And, landing pages are often used for lead generation with some sort of free incentive to opt in or subscribe. The sending of follow-up emails or "nurture sequences" (a series of emails) is usually automated for each lead to tell a story, build loyalty, and promote an offer.

▶ ClickFunnels is one of many landing page and sales funnel builder platforms for coaches, authors, marketers, and other entrepreneurs.

SELF-EMPLOYMENT

- Leadpages is another platform which Jim prefers and has personally used for his clients. He recommends it for bloggers with existing sites because the Leadpages plugin will easily integrate landing pages with the sites permalink structure.
- Instapage and Thrive offer comparable capabilities.

Perhaps your business model is to focus on a specific conversion process. If you plan to sell one specific product or service, and don't want to maintain additional regularly updated content on your website, consider these platforms and tools for building your sales funnel and landing pages. Most platforms feature integrated e-commerce, email marketing and customer management solutions. Descriptions are provided by each platform.

SALES FUNNEL & PAGE BUILDERS

ClickFunnels
https://www.clickfunnels.com
Quickly create beautiful sales funnels that convert your visitors Into leads and then customers.

Leadpages
https://www.leadpages.com
Leadpages helps small businesses connect with an audience, collect leads, and close sales. Integrate landing pages seamlessly with your WordPress website with the Leadpages plugin.

Instapage
https://instapage.com
Where conversion happens. Instapage includes six products and hundreds of features built specifically to help you increase your advertising conversion rates.

Landingi
https://landingi.com
Landingi's simple drag and drop page builder lets you quickly create, launch, and optimize unlimited campaigns – so you can turn more traffic into revenue.

Convertkit
https://convertkit.com
The creator marketing platform. Whatever you make, make it known with ConvertKit.

Unbounce
https://unbounce.com
Build landing pages and optimize your marketing campaigns with conversion intelligence.

WishPond
https://www.wishpond.com
Reach new customers and increase sales, affordably. WishPond is an all-in-one marketing platform you need to grow your business and a team of experts doing the work for you.

Pagewiz
https://www.pagewiz.com
Scale up your paid campaigns with the ultimate landing page platform.

Hubspot
https://www.hubspot.com
HubSpot's CRM platform has all the tools and integrations you need for marketing, sales, content management, and customer service.

WORDPRESS LANDING PAGE THEMES/PLUGINS

Thrive Architect
https://thrivethemes.com/architect
The WordPress theme framework for creating smart landing pages, Thrive is a revolutionary new way of creating landing pages on your WordPress website.

Elementor
https://elementor.com
From landing pages, and e-commerce stores, to full-blown websites – build it all with Elementor.

SeedProd
https://www.seedprod.com
A WordPress landing page plugin that's fast and easy.

BeaverBuilder
https://www.wpbeaverbuilder.com
Awesome software, great support, and a helpful community. Beaver Builder is the WordPress page builder you can trust with your business.

Divi
https://www.elegantthemes.com/gallery/divi
The most popular WordPress theme in the world and the ultimate WordPress page builder.

Kadence Theme
https://www.kadencewp.com/kadence-theme
Built from the ground up for lightning-fast performance, yet filled with modern features that will make building websites fun again.

OptimizePress
https://www.optimizepress.com
OptimizePress is a complete WordPress tools suite that helps you create pages & funnels that grow your list and make more sales.

Email Marketing and List Management

The growth of your business depends upon growing your contact list. While many sales funnel platforms and landing page builders have integrated list management and email marketing tools, some require integration with third party software. Or, you may have a WordPress website and need a solution for growing your list and sending email campaigns. We've used Mailchimp for years to manage our email list and create opt-in forms on our Tripawds landing pages (built with WordPress).

Mailchimp is great platform for getting started in email marketing. It offers a free plan, but with some serious limitations. Premium plans allow for more than 2000 subscribers and include advanced features. These include the ability to send "customer journey" automation sequences, schedule sending of email campaigns, and create A/B split testing to evaluate response rates and performance. Such advanced features, plus list segmentation, and on demand support are recommended for serious email marketers.

Below are some leading email marketing platforms to consider, if your chosen funnel/page builder platform does not include such built-in functionality.

EMAIL MARKETING PLATFORMS
Mailchimp
https://mailchimp.com
Engage your customers and boost your business with Mailchimp's advanced, yet easy-to-use marketing platform.

Constant Contact
https://www.constantcontact.com
Grow an audience for your small business, send awesome emails, create social ads, and sell online with our all-in-one digital marketing platform.

Sendinblue
https://www.sendinblue.com
A multi-faceted solution including email marketing. Promote your brand and grow your business with beautifully designed emails.

Drip
https://www.drip.com
Email and SMS marketing for growing e-commerce brands. Run sophisticated multi-channel marketing campaigns that are proven to drive more sales - all with zero coding skills required.

ConvertKit
https://convertkit.com
The email marketing tool designed for creators. ConvertKit helps you connect with your audience and grow your business using email marketing software that's so easy to use.

AWeber
https://www.aweber.com
Powerfully-simple email marketing designed to help your small business grow - now for free.

ActiveCampaign
https://www.activecampaign.com
ActiveCampaign gives you the email marketing, marketing automation, and CRM tools you need to create incredible customer experiences.

Moosend
https://moosend.com
The fastest path from email marketing to business growth. Build smart email campaigns that drive results.

EmailOctopus
https://emailoctopus.com
Email marketing made easy. Simple, powerful tools to grow your business. Easy to use, quick to master and all at an affordable price.

Omnisend
https://www.omnisend.com
Take the shortcut to revenue growth with Omnisend's easy-to-use platform for e-commerce email marketing, SMS and automation.

MailJet
https://www.mailjet.com
Build together. Send smarter. Grow your business with meaningful emails.

MailerLite
https://www.mailerlite.com
Take email marketing beyond the inbox with advanced tools made easy. Enjoy award-winning live 24/7 support along with all the features you need to succeed.

GetResponse
https://www.getresponse.com
Powerful, simplified tool to send emails, create pages, and automate your marketing.

Yikes Easy Forms for Mailchimp
(WordPress Plugin)
https://yikesplugins.com/plugin/mailchimp-wordpress-plugin
Easily build unlimited forms for your Mailchimp lists, add them to your site. (Mailchimp account required.)

Enter the World of Self-Publishing

Finally, one of the best ways to profit from your expertise is to sell information products and publish your own books. Self-publishing is the smart way to publish any book, and many platforms help simplify production, distribution, and marketing. In rare cases, if your subject matter is topical and trendy, you may be able to land a deal with a major traditional publishing house, with or without the help of a literary agent. But unless you know somebody in the industry, landing a traditional publishing contract can be tricky and time consuming. Oftentimes, publishers claim exclusive copyright to the content you worked so hard to develop. This may leave you with no rights to your intellectual property should you wish to publish elsewhere. Most publishers also leave the marketing up to the authors, providing little or no promotional support for titles that are not immediately wildly successful.

How to find a self-publishing partner

There are many companies that offer self-publishing packages to help authors get their books into the marketplace. Most offer print-on-demand production, saving authors the expense of bulk printing books that may end up in the closet. Writers Digest has a comprehensive <u>Directory of Self-Publishing Companies</u> with detailed information about each. Writers who may need help with design, production, and marketing should consider sourcing assistance from the various talent marketplaces we've listed previously. Or, consider working with a full service firm that provides self-publishing packages such as <u>Xlibris</u> or <u>MindStir Media</u>.

For authors who wish to retain total control of the publishing process, leading platforms for DIY self-publishing include Amazon's <u>Kindle Direct Publishing</u>, <u>Ingram Spark</u>, <u>Lulu Press</u>, <u>Blurb</u>, and <u>BookBaby</u>. Most platforms also distribute books to Amazon, in addition to their own marketplaces. Many self-published authors choose to publish directly on the world's largest marketplace to take advantage of Amazon's KDP Select promotional tools and features. It is important to note, however, that publishing your e-books using KDP Select requires agreement to their exclusivity terms.

> *[With] KDP Select, you're committing to make the digital format of that book available exclusively through KDP. During the period of exclusivity, you cannot distribute your book digitally anywhere else, including on your website, blogs, etc.*
> – <u>KDP SELECT TERMS AND CONDITIONS</u>

@liveworkdream

One easy option for new authors is Blurb. The Blurb platform specializes in short-run production of premium quality photo books and offers various premium paper and binding options. Our Blurb Bookstore features a couple of limited edition photo books and a special magazine style guide-book we created for Tripawds fans.

We use our Tripawds Lulu Store to cost effectively produce and distribute our annual Tripawds calendars with print-on-demand publishing.

If you want your book to be sold in bricks and mortar bookstores, consider also using Ingram Spark. Retail bookstores around the world purchase their inventory from the Ingram catalog. Bookstore purchasing agents are less likely to purchase from Amazon. Jim wrote about why and how we self-publish our books using KDP and Ingram in his Live Work Dream blog post, Self Publishing on the Road.

This is not intended to be a how-to guide on self-publishing. That's an entire book on itself, and there are plenty of those available. There are, however, important things you need to know before diving into production of your first book. Things like what is an ISBN, and why you should purchase your own, or the tools available for generating the different e-book formats.

One of the most helpful books we read when publishing *Be More Dog*, was APE – Author Publisher Entrepreneur. This classic by entrepreneurial guru Guy Kawasaki is an essential read for any author interested which covers all the basics about self-publishing.

Below you will find additional resources and a few of the leading self-publishing platforms, all of which have extensive tutorials and documentation.

SELF PUBLISHING PLATFORMS & AGENCIES

Kindle Direct Publishing (Amazon)
https://kdp.amazon.com
Self-publish e-books and paperbacks for free with Kindle Direct Publishing, and reach millions of readers on Amazon.

Ingram Spark
https://www.ingramspark.com
Ingram Spark offers global book distribution and free resources to help you self-publish successfully.

Lulu Book Printing and Publishing
https://www.lulu.com
Lulu has the right tools for authors, publishers, and businesses to fulfill all your book printing needs.

Blurb
https://www.blurb.com
Summon your creative superpowers for photography, storytelling, recipe inventing, and more into meaningful, bookstore-quality gifts. View the Tripawds Blurb Bookstore:
https://www.blurb.com/user/agreda

BookBaby
https://www.bookbaby.com
Where Writers Become Authors. Self-publishing services for every step of your journey.

Luminare Press
https://www.luminarepress.com
Luminare Press offers hybrid print on demand publishing services: Cover designs, interior formatting, e-books, marketing, and more.

Xlibris
https://www.xlibris.com
Xlibris guides you all the way: Publishing Packages, Editorial Services, Add-On Services, and Marketing Services

MindStir Media
https://mindstirmedia.com
MindStir Media is an award-winning self-publishing company offering Mind-Stirringly Easy Book Publishing.

Writers Digest Self Publishing Directory
https://www.writersdigest.com/get-published-sell-my-work/directory-of-self-publishing-companies

RECOMMENDED READING
APE – How to Publish a Book, Author Publisher Entrepreneur
https://amzn.to/3Je9FNq

Self Publishing for Dummies
https://amzn.to/3yJOGy7

14 Steps to Self-Publishing a Book
https://amzn.to/32jA4cv

Kindle Publishing Made (Stupidly) Easy
https://amzn.to/3Ekbq8N

Self-publishing a book: 25 things you need to know
https://www.cnet.com/tech/services-and-software/self-publishing-a-book-25-things-you-need-to-know/

The Best 101 on Self-Publishing + Resources
https://www.writersdigest.com/general/the-best-101-on-self-publishing-resources

Self Publishing on the Road
https://liveworkdream.com/2019/12/06/self-publishing-on-the-road

> *Writing a book isn't an easy process nor is it always enjoyable, but it is one of life's most satisfying achievements."*
>
> – GUY KAWASAKI

CONCLUSION

Yes, You Can Design Your Own Nomadic Lifestyle!

Follow your passion, find purpose, and you will do well in life. That's the gist of something we learned from reading <u>Deepak Chopra</u> long ago. Dr. Chopra basically believes:

- Do what you love, and you will do it well.
- Do it well and you will be rewarded, both financially and emotionally.

Our fifteen plus years on the road doing what we love is proof that Chopra's insight is true. We began following his words of wisdom when we first launched our little marketing firm in the remote Northern California redwoods. We succeeded with our early business endeavors because we love helping business owners find the right solution to meet their needs and reach their goals. We've continued our personal growth and financial fulfillment ever since <u>hitting the road with Jerry</u>, and discovering our purpose for the work we do at Tripawds.

We hope this book helps you follow your dreams, too. If your goal is to live the nomadic lifestyle, we trust you've learned some tips for making the transition. If you're looking for remote employment, we wish you the best of luck finding that perfect job using the resources we provided. And no matter what talents you have, if you want to make some side hustle money, hopefully you've discovered there's an app for that.

Finally – whether you're a coach or a carpenter – if you're anything like us, you'd rather be your own boss. We hope you now have the inspiration and direction to start growing your own location independent business!

CONCLUSION

We understand that what works for some may be difficult for others. What we do to support our lifestyle might not be right for you. At the very least, we hope that our story will inspire you to live your own life to the fullest. After all, if we can live our dreams, so can you!

Just remember: as <u>Dave Ramsey</u> says, **"The difference between a dream and a goal is a plan."** You took the first step to fulfilling your dreams by reading this book. Hopefully you've taken lots of notes and bookmarked many websites. Your next step is to put some of these things you've learned into action. Whether it was steps for getting out of debt, how to start a side gig, or ways to monetize your blog, now is the time to make it so!

What's Your Next Move?

If you are a full-time RVer or want to be, <u>learn more about workamping</u>. Want to supplement your income? Join the Gig Economy. And if it's time to turn that crazy idea into your new business, ask yourself, <u>Will it Fly?</u>

Whatever you decide to do, don't wait. If the global pandemic taught humanity anything, it's that life is unpredictable. Don't fall sick with Someday Syndrome. If you want to follow your dreams, there is no better time than **Now** to pursue them.

> *If you don't like the road you're walking, start paving another one.*
> – DOLLY PARTON

> *The road goes on forever, but the party never ends...*
> – ROBERT EARL KEEN, JR.

Somewhere Near Marfa Texas
https://liveworkdream.com/tag/marfa

Yes, you can live a life untethered from debt and traditional employment. What are you waiting for?

We Want to Hear from You!

Tell us what you want out of your new work-from-anywhere lifestyle. What steps have you taken to make it happen? Send us your story of struggle or success. Ask us any questions about RVing or making money on the road. We'll consider sharing them with our Live Work Dream readers and sending you a little social love.

LET'S CONNECT
Subscribe to Live Work Dream
https://liveworkdream.com/subscribe

Facebook: @LiveWorkDream
https://Facebook.com/liveworkdream/

Twitter: @LiveWorkDream
https://twitter.com/liveworkdream/

Instagram: @LiveWorkDream
https://instagram.com/liveworkdream/

LinkedIn: Jim Nelson
https://www.linkedin.com/in/jcnjr/

INTERESTED IN WORKAMPING?
All About Workamping:
https://liveworkdream.com/workamping

Workamper News Details and Promo Code:
https://bit.ly/wknpromo

Workampers Facebook Group
https://www.Facebook.com/groups/weloveworkamping/

Happy Travels!

RENE AGREDANO & JIM NELSON
Creators, Live Work Dream: https://liveworkdream.com

Authors, Be More Dog: https://bemoredog.net

Founders, Tripawds https://tripawds.com

APPENDIX

Questions To Ask About Your Workamping Job

The following list of questions to ask potential workamping employers was compiled by members of the Facebook Workampers group.

Workamping questions about the work you'll do:

- What are your job requirements? Is there a written job description for the position?
- What are the start and end dates? Can you arrive early or stay late at no cost, and if so for how long?
- Exactly, what does "light maintenance" include?
- What does "some grounds work" really entail?
- As a workamper, will you greet campers and assign them to their sites, and then just be there to keep an eye on things?
- Will you also be expected to clean bathrooms, cut weeds, and solve problems?
- What type of physical exertion is required of workamping? How long on feet, how much walking, heavy lifting, etc.?
- Can a couple work the same shifts and, receive the same consecutive days off?
- Are all tools and equipment provided?
- Will we be expected to be "on call" during off hours?

Questions about the campground or RV park:

- Where is the campground facility?
- What do they mean by "centrally located" (if applicable)?
- Where is the workamper site located and what size is it?
- Are there full hookups and does my site have 30A or 50A electric service?
- Can we receive mail and packages at the park?

- If 55+ park, can workampers be younger than 55?
- Is there a uniform issued and/or clothing requirement?
- What park amenities or recreational facilities or equipment will we have access to use on days off?
- Can we wash/wax our RV/car at the site?
- Any "local" discounts provided?
- What is the best way to approach the park in a big RV?

Questions about the social climate of the park:

- Are there many organized activities?
- Is it adult orientated or billed as a family vacation spot?
- Are most of the guests overnighters or are they staying for the season?

Workamping questions about your pay or benefits:

- How will you be compensated?
- If you are working in exchange for a site, is it possible to work extra hours for a salary?
- Is it mandatory that you work additional hours when the park is busy?
- How many hours will you be expected to work each week in exchange for the campsite?
- Is that per couple or per person?
- Will it be in a concentrated period of time, such as two full days?
- Or, will it be spread out, a couple hours every day?
- Will you work weekends or have weekends off?
- If free use of the facility's amenities is included, what are those park amenities?
- Will you be issued a 1099 or W2?

Miscellaneous Workamping Questions:

- Is laundry facility available, and is any credit provided for free use? Or, how far is nearest laundromat?
- Is propane available on site, and is any credit provided for filling tanks? Or, how far is nearest propane?
- How far is the nearest post office, pharmacy, hospital, supermarket, bank, gas station, etc.?
- Is there reliable WiFi at my RV site? Any restricted use?
- How is the cellular service at my location? (Ask about your specific Carrier!)
- If you have satellite internet or TV service: Does my site have clear view of the southern sky?
- Is there an age restriction on the types of RVs allowed?
- Are meals, store credit, or any other alternative compensation provided?
- Are children welcome? Can my teenagers work?
- Are pets allowed? Any dog breed restrictions?
- Can workamping parents request separate shifts to care for young ones at home?

Questions to Ask Yourself

- How bad do I want to visit this area?
- What might I learn on the job?
- What challenges might we face taking this job?
- Can we commit to the full length of stay?
- Do I personally consider the arrangement a fair deal? (Ignore what others say based only on payment.)

Have additional questions or suggestions? Edit this list to help improve it for others! See the Files tab in the <u>Facebook Workampers Group</u>:

<u>https://www.face-book.com/notes/workampers/questions-to-ask-about-your-campground-host-job/971770109571419/</u>

Pyramid Style Schemes vs. Legitimate Revenue Sharing Businesses

Considering participating in an MLM or product marketing business? The chart below presents considerations that can save you from getting scammed.

Legitimate Revenue Sharing Businesses	Poorly Run MLM Programs and Pyramid Scams
The company makes money from selling real products to actual consumers who use them.	The company profits from people buying into the business.
The majority of the company's customers are involved to take advantage of savings on products they actually use.	Everyone who participates in the program is involved only to make money from operating a business.
Repeat business is practically guaranteed; customer attrition never exceeds 5 to 10%.	Keeping repeat customers is difficult; MLM businesses typically have an attrition rate of up to 70%.
The company carries a large selection of common products to choose from, such as consumables readily available elsewhere.	The company promotes a specific "Miracle Product" or very narrow product line – vitamins, juice drink, magnet wrist band, etc.
The company offers savings on real products, encouraging repeat customers to shop every month.	Products are priced outlandishly high causing discerning customers to shy away.
There is no "upline" or "downline"; everyone in the organization is rewarded equally and nobody's business will ever be "split" when one member's sales exceeds another.	The company punishes business partners whose enrollees (those "below" them in the organizational chart) succeed faster than they do, by splitting the organization up.
Company invests greatly in product development to create clinically proven products backed by scientific studies.	The company makes extraordinary, unbelievable, unscientific product claims.

APPENDIX

Legitimate Revenue Sharing Businesses	Poorly Run MLM Programs and Pyramid Scams
The company requires no startup cost, or a minimal enrollment fee, and handles all customer relations directly. Business partners have no sales quotas other than goals they set for themselves.	Business partners must pay a large upfront investment and usually must carry inventory and process orders, often with a quota to stock up every month.
The company rewards everyone in any business partner's organization equally based upon their individual performance.	Compensation model is based on timing of when someone "got in" as opposed to how many purchases from end consumers they actually generated. Money is funneled to the top of the pyramid where the first guy wins and the last guy in loses.
Million dollar business within the company are run by dedicated executives who have been working in the company for many years.	The opportunity is promoted as a "get rich quick" scheme with catch phrases like "two-year retirement" or "Six Figure Income in Six Weeks".
The company offers a 100% satisfaction guaranty on all their products, while allowing business partners to cancel within a given time frame and get all their money back.	The company offers no satisfaction guarantee on their products, and will not refund enrollment fees to dissatisfied business partners.
All sales are driven by actual demand for real products from repeat customers.	Sales volumes are created by promotions and incentives to "invest" in the program.
The company is totally transparent, providing detailed company statistics and business income reports to all business partners.	The company does not disclose where they are based, hides financial reports and does not disclose what their distributors make at all levels.

Recommended Reading

Mindset

The Seven Spiritual Laws of Success
https://amzn.to/3mlmn3N

Atomic Habits: An Easy & Proven Way to Build Good Habits & Break Bad Ones
https://amzn.to/3A1iU01

Be More Dog: Learning to Live in the Now
https://bemoredog.net

Finances & Planning

Your Money or Your Life: 9 Steps to Transforming Your Relationship with Money and Achieving Financial Independence
https://amzn.to/3FvQrBi

Smart Couples Finish Rich, Revised and Updated: 9 Steps to Creating a Rich Future for You and Your Partner
https://amzn.to/3yMY18a

The Total Money Makeover
https://amzn.to/3qnMrwK

Business & Entrepreneurship

48 Days to the Work You Love
https://amzn.to/3F4VPei

Will It Fly?
https://amzn.to/3eYmFK1

APE: Author Publisher Entrepreneur
https://amzn.to/3G6Jxmo

RVing and Workamping

Can I Write Off my RV?
https://amzn.to/3kHphPA

Workamper News
https://workamper.com/register-new-workamper

Find the best workamping jobs in Workamper News with promo code AGRE6207!
Details at: https://bit.ly/wknpromo

ALSO FROM LIVEWORKDREAM & TRIPAWDS FOUNDERS
RENE AGREDANO & JIM NELSON:

Be More Dog: Learning to Live in the Now

Enjoying Every Day to the Fullest on the Road to Happiness

"I love that they got in the RV and did it for their dog, Jerry."
– OPRAH WINFREY (THE GAYLE KING SHOW, MAY 2010)

Be More Dog is the inspiring story of how one dog with terminal cancer led his people on a spiritual journey that turned their life around and opened their eyes to the importance of living in the Now.

Be More Dog is more than a memoir about a three-legged dog on an epic road trip. It is a mantra to live by, and this book is the guide.

This heartwarming tale is filled with deep meaning. Through his actions and attitude in the face of adversity, Jerry shows Jim and Rene how important it is to live in the now – to persevere when the going gets tough, to never give up, and that every day is a great day, no matter what life throws your way.

Through telling Jerry's story, they share details from their early workamping experiences, and how they turned their passion into a full-time labor of love that continues to support their nomadic lifestyle 15+ years later.

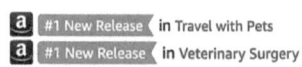

With foreword by MUTTS creator Patrick McDonnell!

Available everywhere books are sold.
Find special gift edition and bonus material at:
https://bemoredog.net

Made in United States
Troutdale, OR
03/29/2025